797,885 Books

are available to read at

Forgotten Books

www.ForgottenBooks.com

Forgotten Books' App
Available for mobile, tablet & eReader

ISBN 978-0-243-23697-8
PIBN 10262457

This book is a reproduction of an important historical work. Forgotten Books uses state-of-the-art technology to digitally reconstruct the work, preserving the original format whilst repairing imperfections present in the aged copy. In rare cases, an imperfection in the original, such as a blemish or missing page, may be replicated in our edition. We do, however, repair the vast majority of imperfections successfully; any imperfections that remain are intentionally left to preserve the state of such historical works.

Forgotten Books is a registered trademark of FB &c Ltd.
Copyright © 2017 FB &c Ltd.
FB &c Ltd, Dalton House, 60 Windsor Avenue, London, SW19 2RR.
Company number 08720141. Registered in England and Wales.

For support please visit www.forgottenbooks.com

1 MONTH OF FREE READING

at

www.ForgottenBooks.com

By purchasing this book you are eligible for one month membership to ForgottenBooks.com, giving you unlimited access to our entire collection of over 700,000 titles via our web site and mobile apps.

To claim your free month visit:

www.forgottenbooks.com/free262457

* Offer is valid for 45 days from date of purchase. Terms and conditions apply.

English
Français
Deutsche
Italiano
Español
Português

www.forgottenbooks.com

Mythology Photography **Fiction**
Fishing Christianity **Art** Cooking
Essays Buddhism Freemasonry
Medicine **Biology** Music **Ancient Egypt** Evolution Carpentry Physics
Dance Geology **Mathematics** Fitness
Shakespeare **Folklore** Yoga Marketing
Confidence Immortality Biographies
Poetry **Psychology** Witchcraft
Electronics Chemistry History **Law**
Accounting **Philosophy** Anthropology
Alchemy Drama Quantum Mechanics
Atheism Sexual Health **Ancient History**
Entrepreneurship Languages Sport
Paleontology Needlework Islam
Metaphysics Investment Archaeology
Parenting Statistics Criminology
Motivational

FIRST ANNUAL REPORT

OF THE

TRUSTEES

OF THE

HOLTON LIBRARY,

BRIGHTON,

FEBRUARY 1st, 1865.

BOSTON:
CHARLES H. CROSBY, PRINTER,
Nos. 11 & 13 WATER STREET.
1865.

FIRST ANNUAL REPORTS,

OF THE

TRUSTEES

OF THE

HOLTON LIBRARY,

BRIGHTON,

FEBRUARY 1st, 1865.

BOSTON:
CHARLES H. CROSBY, PRINTER,
Nos. 11 & 13 WATER STREET.
1865.

150,622
Jan. 7, 1874.

FIRST ANNUAL REPORT

OF THE

TRUSTEES OF THE HOLTON LIBRARY.

It seems especially proper that the Trustees of the Holton Library should commence their first Annual Report with a brief notice of its founder. The following biographical sketch has been prepared by the Rev. Frederic A. Whitney, in accordance with a vote of the Board.

JAMES HOLTON was born in Brighton, then the south part of Cambridge, Thursday, April 10,* 1800, oldest child of Major Benjamin and Mary (Shed) Holton, and died there unmarried, the last of his family, at the estate inherited from his father, on Faneuil Street, but which had not been his birthplace, Wednesday, April 29, 1863, aged sixty-three years and nineteen days.

The benignant countenance and the silver locks of his father, Major Holton, as he was designated, will be long remembered by most of our citizens as he appeared in our streets, and in his pew at the First Church, forenoon and afternoon, until he had reached

---

* On page 3, Rules and Regulations Holton Library, substitute April 10 for April 12, as his birthday. The same error may be corrected in a notice of his family on page 21 "Champney Genealogy." Also, in connection with this error in the Genealogy, the date of his father's marriage should read May 3, 1799, *not* May 2, 1779, and the name of his grandmother should be Hephzibah, *not* Mary.

nearly fourscore years. He, also, was a native of this place, having been born here on Washington Street, north side, near Allston Street, in a house which stood on the present site of Mr. Horace Jordan's house, February 13, 1775, son of James Holton and Rebecca (Brown) Champney, widow of Solomon Champney. Solomon Champney, grandfather of our Selectman, Mr. William Champney, having been accidentally killed here, by falling from his team, April 3, 1763, his widow married, January 2, 1766, James Holton, who died here April 16, 1789, aged 60. She was of New Ipswich, N. H.; was admitted Communicant of the First Church here, then the Third Church of Cambridge. March 27, 1785, and died in the family of her son, Mr. Nathaniel Champney, with whom she had lived several years a widow, October 27, 1805, aged 71 years.

James Holton, the grandfather of our donor, came to this country from Scotland. He married for his first wife, Jerusha Blake, daughter of John Blake, of Boston, and Susanna Smith, of Cambridge. From the tattered leaves of an old Bible of the Blake family, which came into the possession of the Holton family, I transcribe these fragmentary entries:—

John Blake and Susanna Smith were married Feb. the ——.
Jerusha Blake and James Holton were married July 4, 1756.
Mr. John Blake departed this life March the 20th, 1756, and was buried 25th day.
Jerusha Blake,—her book being the gift of her mother,—May 20, 1756.
Mrs. Susanna Blake died April 2–, and was buried 26th day.
Jerusha Holton departed this life August 11, 1764, aged 29, and was buried 15th.
February 12, 1772, Rebecca Holton was born, daughter of James.
Nathan Champney, son to James and Rebecca Holton, was born July 18, 1761.

Susanna Smith, (Mrs. John Blake, of Boston,) was sister to Mr. Ebenezer Smith, of this place, (son of Henry and Lydia (Buck) Smith, of Cambridge,) a man of very large estate, who died here unmarried, September 11, 1776, aged 85, whose tomb and monumental inscription may be seen in our old burying-ground. By his will he made numerous bequests; to this section of the town of Cambridge, wood-land for school purposes; to the First Parish here, a parsonage estate on corner of Washington and Rockland Streets, and also a legacy in money; to various individuals here and elsewhere, portions of his ample real and personal estate. A particular notice of him may be found in the School Committee's Report, 1861. Lydia, a daughter of John and Susanna (Smith) Blake, and sister of Jerusha (Blake) Holton, became the first wife of Nathaniel Sparhawk, father of our Patriarch, Mr. Edward Sparhawk, who is still with us, in his 95th year, sound in mind and body, and often in our streets. His mother was his father's second wife, Hannah, daughter of John Murdock, of Newton. Through the Blake family, the connection between the Holtons and Sparhawks is thus traced.

James Holton, grandfather of the subject of our notice, resided at one time in a house which stood far up on Rockland Street, and off the road, near the Brookline boundary, and was reached by a lane running to it from the south side of the street, at the termination of the large ledge of rocks. So retired was this house, that it became subsequently a hospital for patients vaccinated for the small-pox. Though taken down many years since, the cellar may be still seen. He resided afterwards on Washington Street, in the house above described, near Allston Street. This house, with a barn, and about one acre and three-quarters, was a bequest, by the tenth clause of Mr. Ebenezer Smith's will, to James Holton, who, as we have seen, had married for his first wife, Mr. Smith's niece, and to Thomas Thwing, Mr. Smith's nephew, son of Edward Thwing and Lydia Smith. The estate is bounded in the will, southerly on the county road; westerly and northerly on land of Abijah Learned; easterly on land of Samuel Phipps. The Holton and Thwing families occupied the house. The two noble elm trees which stand at this day, the pride of the street, in front of the house now on the old cellar, were planted entirely by the hands of Mrs. Holton, the second wife, and Mrs. Thwing. These trees, it is said, were, in consequence, long distinguished by the neighbors and friends of the families, each by the name of the lady who planted it.

In this house, James Holton the elder died, in 1789, and here his son Benjamin, the Major, was born, as we have seen, in 1775. I find on the church records, married here May 19, 1794, Mr. Oliver Gerry and Miss Rebecca Holton. She was sister to Benjamin. James, the donor, makes bequests in his will to her children, his cousins. Major Holton, when a young man, was in the employ of Mr. Jonathan Winship, of this place, who was very extensively engaged in business, and who built and occupied the large house on Washington Street, at its junction with Cambridge Street, now the Brighton Hotel. Here Mr. Holton lived, and here he was doubtless in the habit of meeting the lady whom he married, Miss Mary Shed, of Roxbury, Mr. Winship's niece. She was born in Roxbury, Feb. 9, 1777, daughter of Thomas Shed and Hephzibah Winship. Her father lived on the corner of what was then called Mather's Lane; and, a few years before his death, removed to Portland, Me., to reside with a son who had settled there.

Benjamin was married in this place by Rev. Dr. Foster, May 3, 1799, and began his wedded life in the house on Washington Street, north side, now owned and occupied by Mr. Jesse Osborn, the first house east from the First Church. This venerable building, one of the oldest in town, was formerly the Fessenden Estate. Here all the children of Benjamin Holton, except the youngest son, were born, while all, with both their parents, died at their subsequent home on Faneuil Street. It is hoped that the Trustees may present in their next Report, for preservation, engravings of this building and of the birthplace, and also of the beautiful monument erected at Evergreen Cemetery to the memory of Mr. Holton. The names of the children follow.

James, born April 10, 1800, died April 29, 1863. Charles, born October 22, 1802, died February 15, 1854, unmarried. Mary Winship, born February 9, 1805, married at Concord, N. H., March 4,

1845, Aaron Colby, and died October 29, 1851, without children. Her husband died at Concord, about 1861. Benjamin, born March 7, 1807, died November 14, 1826, unmarried. The Act of Incorporation making Brighton a town set off from Cambridge, was passed in the Legislature on the last day of February, 1807, and the population of this place being then very small, it chanced that Benjamin, the youngest son, was always distinguished as the first child born in the town.

Major Holton first purchased the old house, which had been Deacon Hill's, still standing on Faneuil Street, north side, second from Market Street, and moved into it in 1805. His latter residence on the same side of the street, second east from Parsons Street, he purchased in 1813. Here Mrs. Holton died Sunday, April 28, 1844, in her 68th year, much beloved for her practical benevolence and the kindly qualities of her heart. She was interred on the 30th. Her husband died Friday, April 15, 1853, in his 79th year, and was interred on the 18th. His hoary head was the crown of glory, because found in the way of righteousness. In such universal esteem was he held, that a very large concourse of the citizens attending his funeral, followed in procession on foot, after the early custom of New England, to the family tomb on Market Street.

Thus in the short space of nine years, the venerable father and mother, the brother and sister, had died, following the youngest born and earliest taken, and James was left alone. He still occupied the paternal estate, having a housekeeper, and cultivated the farm, distributing, often, of its stores to the needy.

His residence was always in this town. He was not much in places of public resort, but mostly at home. His health, in later years, had been somewhat impaired, and he would frequently make short excursions upon the sea, sharing the labors of the sailor's life, which he enjoyed, and by which he was sensibly benefited. His will, in thirty-three articles, bears date July 2, 1855, a little more than two years after his father's decease, with a codicil in four articles appended, July 24, 1860. His property, in part inherited, was principally amassed by his own diligence, honesty and wise economy. Through the courtesy of the Executor, Mr. Life Baldwin, the will has been printed and distributed among those interested. "The Seamen's Bethel Relief Society," Boston, now under the pastoral care of Rev. Edward T. Taylor, is made Residuary Legatee of his large estate, after the settlement of his just debts and funeral charges, the erection of a tomb and monument at Evergreen Cemetery, in this town, and the payment of nearly sixty thousand dollars ($60,000) in legacies. These legacies are embraced in the foundation for the Public Library; in bequests for the Sabbath Schools and Benevolent Sewing Circles of Religious Societies in this town; in a permanent fund for furnishing Thanksgiving-day dinners to the Town paupers, and in another fund for furnishing the same to needy families in town; in bequests to numerous relatives and friends here and elsewhere; to the Boston Port Society, to the Farm School, and to the Ladies' American Home Education and Temperance Society, Boston. The fund which will accrue to the Residuary Legatee, on the final settlement of the estate, cannot yet be known, but must be very ample.

In enumerating this judicious distribution of Mr. Holton's property, we have sufficiently established his benevolence. He always loved especially to help the deserving poor and needy; while he would often refuse aid to many really worthy causes not of this class, and thus, in the estimation of some, damage his generosity. The amount of money which he thus gave in small sums, where it would tell directly on human relief, was each year very large, as shown by his journal. But for the leaves of that accurate journal, the world might never have known how much he did. In heart, and spirit, in manners, in dress, he was opposed to all ostentation. It was his delight that his alms were in secret. Probably no one but the lawyer who drew his will knew of this liberal array of bequests. The deeds of his right hand his left hand knew not. Beneath an almost repulsive plainness of exterior was a heart that beat for the welfare and happiness of his fellow creatures, and, we believe, was right with God. His honesty and integrity were above reproach. Regular and methodical in business, strictly temperate in his habits, a man of few words, unassuming, diffident, he passed a quiet and uneventful life. For most of his life he was a constant attendant with his father's family on worship at the First Church here. He subsequently became warmly interested in the ministrations of Rev. Edward T. Taylor,—Father Taylor, as he is usually designated,—of the Seamen's Bethel, Boston, and would frequently worship on one-half, or on the whole of the Sabbath there. He was for several years a generous donor to this religious association, besides constituting it his Residuary Legatee. For its worthy and venerable pastor he entertained a lively affection. His sympathies were strongly enlisted in the cause of seamen, as may be judged from significant expressions in his will. He conferred often with Father Taylor, his friend, and so emphatically their friend, on the best methods of serving them, and was frequently gladdened by the visits of Father Taylor in his own home here.

For six or seven years before his death he was deeply interested in modern Spiritualism. He attended the meetings of the Spiritualists; he argued with fervid honesty and earnestness for their doctrines with his old friends, who, if they could not accept his conclusions and agree with his views, never doubted his sincerity, the kindness of his heart, nor his conscientious love of the right.

It pleased God to remove him from this life without the sufferings of protracted illness. On the afternoon of Tuesday, April 28, 1863, in his usual health and spirits, he took a friend, Mr. J. B. Mason, who had dined with him, and drove to Kenrick's Nurseries in Newton to purchase some trees. As an evidence of his carefulness in accounts, it may be stated that his Executor found entered that evening on his journal the sum paid for the trees. He returned home before sundown, after conveying his friend to the railroad station here for Boston, and retired early to rest, as was his custom. About midnight he arose feeling unwell, probably from some disease of the heart. His housekeeper administered remedies under his advice, as he considered that by observation and experience he had acquired some medical skill. These proving unavailing, a physician was sent for; but before he arrived, Mr. Holton had passed away, at about two o'clock on the morning of the 29th, in full possession of his faculties, sensible that the hour of his departure had come, and in submission and peace.

His funeral was attended from his house on Saturday, at one o'clock, by a large number of citizens. Rev. Mr. Noyes, of the First Church, offered prayer; Rev. Edward T. Taylor made an address; Rev. Mr. Whitney read the Scripture burial-service. The body was laid in the family tomb on Market Street, to be afterwards removed with the remains of all the family, when the tomb, as directed in the will, should be built at Evergreen Cemetery.

In the summer of 1864 the Town appointed Messrs. Ruggles, Whitney, and Bickford, of the Trustees of the Holton Library, a Committee to select a Lot at Evergreen Cemetery to be placed at the disposal of the Executor, whereby he should fulfil the purpose of the testator in the erection of a tomb. On the 29th of July the Committee met at the Cemetery Mr. Charles Heard, Commissioner, and Mr. Baldwin, Executor, and selected the north extremity of South Grove as the Lot. Previously no lots had been assigned for occupancy either in North or South Grove.

Under the supervision of the Executor the tomb was immediately commenced; and in November all the bodies of the Holton family entombed in the old burying-ground were removed to this new tomb, the top of which is level with the Lot, and sealed up forever. The beautiful marble monument of most appropriate design, rising eighteen feet with its massive granite pedestal, and surmounted by the cross and anchor interlaced in carving, was erected Monday, January 30, 1865. This admirable specimen of an art, which the growing taste of New England for ornamental cemeteries has in these latter years greatly fostered, was executed at McDonald's Marble Works, by Mount Auburn. The finely finished granite which forms the edging of the Lot, and the pedestal, was wrought at

Parker's Granite Works, Cambridgeport. The whole tomb, with its embellishments, completed at a cost of over three thousand dollars, reflects the utmost credit upon the Executor, who has so handsomely fulfilled his trust, as well as upon those who wrought.

The following chaste and appropriate inscription, which adorns the front of the monument facing the north, is from the pen of Mr. John Ruggles, chairman of the Committee as above: —

JAMES HOLTON

DIED APR. 29, 1863; AGED 63 YRS.

———o———

The Town of Brighton
expresses its high appreciation
of his integrity and beneficence.
The founder of its Public Library,
and a liberal donor to its Religious
Societies, his name will be ever
associated with its history.
Charitable to the poor, the constant
friend of the Sailor, blessings
will rest upon his tomb.

On the base of the marble monument is carved the following:—

The remains of the Holton family deposited here
and this monument erected in accordance with the
Will of James Holton, by his Executor, Nov. 1864.

And on the base of the granite pedestal is carved in large letters, the family name

HOLTON.

On the eastern side of the monument the names of his parents are inscribed.

BENJAMIN HOLTON

DIED APR. 15, 1853; AGED 78 YRS.

MARY HOLTON

DIED APR. 28, 1844; AGED 67 YRS.

On the western side is inscribed—

BENJAMIN HOLTON, JR.

DIED NOV. 14, 1826; AGED 20 YRS.

MARY W. COLBY

DIED OCT. 29, 1851; AGED 46 YRS.

CHARLES HOLTON

DIED FEB. 15, 1854; AGED 51 YRS.

On the southern side is inscribed the name of an uncle of our donor:

CHARLES SHED

DIED JAN. 30, 1823; AGED 27 YRS.

We close at his tomb this simple sketch of the life of one more benefactor of his race. The wealth which he acquired while living he has left to flow in many channels of usefulness, now that he has died to earth. His good deeds will live after him here. The features of his countenance, his whole personal bearing, his costume, are most perfectly preserved in the admirable life-size portrait which has been executed in the highest style of art, by F. L. Lay, Winter Street, Boston; and by the generosity of Mr. Theodore Matchett, one of the Trustees, adorns the Library. Not less surely will be preserved and perpetuated,—yes, and for ages after painting and canvas shall have faded and crumbled,—every good influence which through his charitable deeds and the books which his liberality has provided, has been wrought. It was hardly to have been expected that one but little familiar with books and human learning should have thus devised both a Public Library for this Town, and a bequest for books for the Farm School, Boston.

Pliny the younger, writing to Tacitus of the death of his uncle, Pliny the elder, says that he deems them happy whom the gods have permitted either to do what is worthy to be written, or to write what is worthy to be read; but most happy those who may do both. " Equidem beatos puto, quibus deorum munere datum est aut facere scribenda, aut scribere legenda; beatissimos vero quibus utrumque." If it was not the gift of our friend to wield the pen for the admiration of mankind, then surely shall his generous deeds be spoken, and written by other hands. Let him be ever remembered gratefully here in the books which his bounty shall supply from year to year. Let them be judiciously selected, tenderly cared for, wisely read. Childhood, youth, and age shall through coming years be established by them in wisdom and truth. And so in them shall be realized that beautiful tribute paid by Cicero, long since, to letters,—" Adolescentiam alunt; senectutem oblectant; secundas res ornant; adversis solatium praebent; delectant domi." Youth they nourish; they make old age pass pleasantly; prosperity they adorn; adversity they solace; home they charm.

The following Articles were inserted in the warrant for the Town Meeting, held March 7, 1864 :—

"Art. 12. To see if the Town will accept a legacy under the will of James Holton, late of Brighton, deceased, and make such arrangements for a Library as will entitle the Town to said legacy, under the provisions of Item 28th of said will, as follows :—

"'Twenty-eighth. I give and bequeath to the inhabitants of the Town of Brighton, in their corporate capacity, and as a corporate body duly established by law, in the county of Middlesex, the sum of six thousand dollars, to be expended in the purchase of books for a public library, for the use of the inhabitants of said Town of Brighton; provided said Town of Brighton shall, within a reasonable time, procure a suitable room and furniture, and appoint a suitable person as librarian, who shall safely keep said books and take care of the same; but if said Town shall refuse to accept this bequest on the above-named terms, then I give and bequeath said six thousand dollars to my residuary legatees hereinafter named.'

"Art. 13. To see what measures, if any, the Town will take for the establishment and maintenance of a Town Library, and for erecting or procuring a suitable building for the same.

"Art. 14. To see if the Town will accept the Library of the Brighton Library Association, upon the terms and conditions contained in Art. 5, Sec. 2, of the Constitution of said corporation, to wit:

"'Art. 5. Sec. 2. The Trustees shall deliver up to the Town of Brighton, or persons authorized by the Town to receive it, the Library and other property of the Association whenever said Town of Brighton shall make suitable provision for the maintenance and increase of the Library; *provided* the Town secure to the Association the Library Room, or some other convenient room, for the meetings of the Association.'"

At the Town Meeting above-mentioned it was

Voted, That a Committee be appointed by the Moderator to take into consideration the whole subject embraced in Articles 12, 13, and 14, and report a course of action for the Town at the next Town Meeting, and report upon all the questions embraced in said Articles; the Committee to consist of seven.

The Moderator, F. L. Winship, Esq., appointed as such Committee, Messrs. John Ruggles, Theodore Matchett, Stephen H. Bennett, Joseph Breck, Granville Fuller, Nathaniel Jackson, and W. D. Bickford.

At the Town Meeting holden April 8, 1864, they submitted the following Report:

"Deeming it a matter of no common importance, that so noble a bequest, and so generous a donation of books should meet with a proper reception by the Town, and that all measures should be taken to carry out the wishes of the donors, and fully to secure the important advantages which we are assured will flow from their liberality, your Committee have made themselves acquainted either by personal examination or by written correspondence with several of the most flourishing libraries in this vicinity. They have inquired into the mode of their establishment, the number and duties of their officers, the condition of their rooms, their rules and regulations, and in general whatever might aid the Town in opening and conducting the important institution proposed. Having held repeated meetings for the interchange of views, your Committee are now prepared unanimously to recommend the adoption of the following Resolutions, which they hereby submit to the Town separately for action thereon.

'1. *Resolved*, That we, legal voters of Brighton, in Town Meeting assembled, gratefully recognizing the public spirit of our late fellow-citizen, Mr. James Holton, hereby accept his munificent bequest; and regarding it as both a pleasing and most important duty, we pledge ourselves faithfully to fulfil his wishes in the trust committed to our charge.

'2. *Resolved*, That we hereby accept of the valuable collection of the Brighton Library Association, with our sincere acknowledgments to the liberal donors.

'3. *Resolved*, That we proceed to the election of twelve Trustees, who shall have charge of the above bequest and donation, establish a Public Library and Reading Room, free, under necessary restrictions, to all the inhabitants of the Town, enact all requisite rules and regulations, appoint a Librarian and Treasurer, select books for the Library, and report their doings at the annual March meeting.

'4. *Resolved*, That the first four on the list of Trustees shall hold office for three years, the second four for two years, and the last four for one year.

'5. *Resolved*, That a Committee be appointed, who shall be empowered to make such alterations in the first story of the Town Hall as to furnish suitable rooms for a Library and Reading Room, and who shall be authorized to procure suitable furniture for the same.

'6. *Resolved*, That the Town Treasurer be authorized to borrow all sums requisite for fitting up and procuring furniture for a Library and Reading Room.

'7. *Resolved*, That the Institution this day established be known by the name of the Holton Library.'"

The foregoing Report was accepted by the Town, and the several Resolutions separately adopted.

The following gentlemen were then elected Trustees:—

Messrs. John Ruggles, Life Baldwin, Theodore Matchett, Stephen H. Bennett, Rev. Frederic A. Whitney, W. D. Bickford, Rev. John P. Cushman, Nathaniel Jackson, W. W. Warren, Joseph A. Pond, Granville Fuller, J. P. C. Winship. Mr. S. H. Bennett having declined the office, Mr. Chas. C. Hutchinson was elected by the Board to fill the vacancy. Mr. Hutchinson having since left the Town, Mr. Bela S. Fiske was chosen in his stead.

The Board of Trustees organized at their first meeting by the choice of John Ruggles as President, and J. P. C. Winship as Secretary. At subsequent meetings Life Baldwin was chosen Treasurer, and J. P. C. Winship Librarian.

One of our first duties was to select suitable rooms for the

Library; and, after some discussion, we decided upon the first story of the Town Hall, on the west side. These rooms have been fitted up and furnished by a Committee of our number, Messrs. Fuller, Matchett, and Jackson, as we flatter ourselves, in a very commodious style. The expense has been somewhat greater than we at first anticipated, but we think we are too well acquainted with the expectations of our fellow-citizens to suppose for a moment that a parsimonious spirit would be approved by them. The Treasurer states the whole amount expended for preparing and furnishing rooms to be $1,133.42. His Report is herewith appended.

A system of Rules and Regulations for the Board of Trustees, and for the use of the Holton Library, has been prepared by a Committee and adopted by the Board, and on application a copy will be furnished to each family.

The time having arrived when it seemed desirable that we should be provided with a Town Seal, Rev. F. A. Whitney, as Committee of the Trustees, procured a device which was accepted by them, and has been approved by the Selectmen of the Town.

The amount received from the bequest of Mr. Holton, after paying the National Tax of five per cent., was $5,700. Of this sum $5,000 have been loaned to the Town Treasurer, at six per cent. interest, and the balance, $700, as also most of the interest which has accrued on the principal of the fund, has been expended for books and periodicals. The whole amount expended for books, including bills not yet paid, is $827.76; for periodicals, estimated, $50; total, $877.76.

The whole number of volumes in the Library is 2,833; number purchased, 729; number deposited by the Town, 37; number received from the High School, 44; number presented by individuals, 73; number presented by the Brighton Library Association, 1,950. This Association was incorporated January 15, 1858, having been established by a number of public-spirited young men of this Town, for the circulation of books, for maintaining courses of public lectures, and for exercises in declamation, composition and debate. With their collection of books was united the Brighton Social Library, organized March 1, 1824. It will be observed that nearly three-fourths of the volumes we now possess were the gift of the Brighton Library Association. For farther information as to the general operation and condition of the Library, we would refer to the appended Report of the Librarian. We would express, in this connection, our gratitude to that officer for his valuable services gratuitously rendered.

In the purchase of books, it has been our aim to promote the improvement of our citizens; and this, not by presenting to them learning and science in their most abstruse and concentrated forms alone, but by mingling the agreeable with the useful; for we are well aware that "all work and no play" is poor philosophy, even for adults. We have had especial regard, too, to the wants of our youth, and have deemed it of the highest importance, not only to encourage in them a love of reading, but to excite a thirst for knowledge, to refine their taste, and especially to advance their moral purity.

The Trustees present their grateful acknowledgments to individuals for gifts to the Library during the past year; especially to Theodore Matchett, Esq., for the excellent portrait of our benefactor which now adorns our rooms; to the same gentleman for "Reports of the Massachusetts Board of Education," in eleven volumes, and the "Rebellion Record," in six volumes; to Hon. Joseph Breck, for "Contributions to the Natural History of the United States," in four volumes, by Agassiz; as also the "Flower Garden," a constant reminder of his own valuable contributions to Horticulture. We hope and trust to have, in future, important accessions to our Library from the donations of our citizens; and we would suggest to those who are interested in any branch of science or the arts, in the culture of the soil or of the mind, not to forget the wants of this our new school for both children and adults.

The Library was opened to the public September 1, for inspection of the room and distribution of the Rules and Regulations, and on the third of the same month for the circulation of books. From that date to the present time it has been very generally patronized, and we cannot but feel that it is a decided success. We have been sometimes surprised, on examining the books taken from the Library, to find so large a proportion of them works of sterling value. We observe also, that some, who in youth have had but little opportunity for improvement, are promising to outstrip those more favored by fortune.

We trust that the Library will be a means of constant self-culture to our citizens, and that in the coming ages it will be a blessing to the Town. In the words of the lamented Everett, written on a similar occasion: "The Library is regarded by the Trustees as the completion of the great system of public education."

While we would urge upon our fellow-citizens the importance of their improving to the utmost their educational advantages, we cannot forget those of our number, who have not for months, and many of them for years, enjoyed the privileges and comforts of home, but who, we are confident, will ere long return to reap the fruits of their toils and dangers. Even now the sun is breaking through the noxious vapors and unwholesome exhalations which have been wafted hither from regions where free schools and free libraries are unknown.

In that glorious future which is opening before us, it will be both the duty and privilege of the Sons of the Pilgrims, to bear these institutions, the fruits of the seeds sown by the Fathers, through the full extent of this broad land, from the lakes to the gulf, and from ocean to ocean.

In behalf of the Trustees,

JOHN RUGGLES, *President.*

January 30, 1865.

REPORT

OF THE

LIBRARIAN OF THE HOLTON LIBRARY.

The Librarian of the Holton Library herewith presents the first report for the year ending January 31.

Upon assuming the charge of the Library in June last, your Librarian caused to be arranged in the manner prescribed by the By-Laws, the volumes transferred from the Brighton Library Association, to which has been added a large number of volumes purchased in accordance with a vote of the Board of Trustees.

The present condition of the Library is as follows :—

Number of volumes received from the Brighton Library Association—
    For circulation, ... 1,904
    For reference, ... 46
                                              1,950

Number of books purchased—
    For circulation, ... 684
    For reference, . . , . . . 45
                                              729

Number of books presented to the Library, . . . 117
Number received from the Selectmen belonging to the Town, 37
Gross number of volumes, exclusive of pamphlets, . . 2,833

Amount appropriated for books,		$700 00
Fines collected,		23 02
Interest accrued to February 1,		166 66
		$889 68
Amount expended for books,	$650 38	
due for books purchased,	177 38	
due for periodicals, about	50 00	
		877 76
Amount in excess unexpended,		$11 92

Number of subscribers,	733
of books taken out since the opening of the Library,	7,691
of days the Library has been open,	38
Average number of books taken out per day,	202

PERIODICALS.

Atlantic Monthly.	Genealogical Register.
Leslie's Magazine.	Scientific American.
Eclectic Magazine.	Harpers' Weekly.
U. S. Service Magazine.	Army and Navy Journal.
Cornhill Magazine.	Littell's Living Age.
Harpers' Magazine.	Punch.
Godey's Magazine.	The Horticulturist.
North American Review.	Our Young Folks' Magazine.

DONATIONS.

Name.	Residence.	Pamphlets.	Vols.
Boutwell, George S. Hon.	Washington, D. C.		9
Breck, Joseph, Hon.	Brighton,		5
Holmes, John H.	Charlestown,		1
Horr, John E.	Brookline,	1	
Johonnot, W. H.	Newton,	5	
Matchett, Theodore,	Brighton, Portrait of Jas. Holton,		20

Name.	Residence.	Pamphlets.	Vols.
Phillips, Samuel, Hon.	Brighton,		1
Pond, Joseph A. Hon.	Brighton,	2	3
Poole, Fitch,	South Danvers,	1	1
Rice, Edmund,	Brighton,		3
Ruggles, John,	Brighton, Engraving of Battle of Gettysburg,		8
Sumner, Charles, Hon.	Washington, D. C.		6
Warren, William,	Brighton,		2
Whitney, F. A. Rev.	Brighton,	55	9
Wight, John B. Rev.	Wayland,	1	
Winship, J. P. C.	Brighton,	2 maps	5

The books called for by young subscribers are generally works of fiction, and thrilling adventures; and a number will read no other kind, refusing to take books unless their taste is satisfied. The question of propriety as to gratifying such tastes is of some moment, but it is a fact that a love for books is frequently first excited by reading such works; and, after becoming satiated, more solid matter is selected.

The periodicals subscribed for were designed for use in the Library, but the present arrangement of the room interfered with that quietness required for reading, and only your intended change can obviate it.

The promiscuous use of the Library has had its effect upon a number of the volumes, especially upon such as have been taken out by the younger portion of the subscribers. In several instances leaves have been torn cut, and the volume so injured as to warrant the charge of maliciousness; and it is hoped that parents will use their influence in this matter, in order to avoid more stringent rules, if possible.

Of the books not returned, a number were taken by transient citizens, and it may be difficult to recover them; others will be restored in time.

Good progress has been made towards preparing a new catalogue, but much labor will be required before it will be ready for the printer.

I have now reason to believe that the Library has become so systematized that a person of ordinary ability can understand the duties required; but the necessity of quickness in the receipt and delivery of books, the attention to fines, and answering the many questions asked, satisfying the disappointed, and quelling any disturbance that may be excited, requires a somewhat able person.

I desire, before closing, to express a kind word in favor of my young assistants, Z. T. Cushman and W. H. Pierce, who have performed the work assigned them faithfully, and with an interest which may aid in their advancement.

All of which is respectfully submitted.

J. P. C. WINSHIP, *Librarian.*

LIFE BALDWIN, as Treasurer, in account with "HOLTON LIBRARY."

Dr.				Cr.
1864. July 5.	To cash received of John Ruggles, Esq., Chairman of the Trustees of "Holton Library,"	$5,700 00	1864. July 9.	By cash paid T. Groom & Co., for Treasurer's book, $1 75
Sept. 15.	To cash received of H. H. Learnard, Town Treasurer, as per order on him, drawn by J. Ruggles, Esq.,	1,125 00		By cash paid J. P. C. Winship, (Librarian) for books as per bills and on file, 665 38
1865. Jan. 3.	To cash received of J. P. C. Winship, for fines paid,	7 00	Oct. 6.	By cash paid for Policy of Insurance on books, 20 00
				By cash paid Messrs. Granville Fuller, and Bro. for sundry bills paid by them for preparing and furnishing a room for the Library, as per bills on file, 1,133 42
				By note against H. H. Learnard as Treasurer of the Town of Brighton, dated July 12th, 1864, 5,000 00
				By cash balance, deposited in Brighton Market Bank, 11 45
		$6,832 00		$6,832 00

This, first account, rendered January 20, 1865,

By L. BALDWIN, *Treasurer of Holton Library.*

To JOHN RUGGLES, Esq., Chairman of the Trustees of Holton Library.

SECOND ANNUAL REPORT

OF THE

TRUSTEES

OF THE

HOLTON LIBRARY,

BRIGHTON,

FEBRUARY 1st, 1866.

BOSTON:
CHARLES H. CROSBY, PRINTER,
Nos. 11 & 13 WATER STREET.
1866.

SECOND ANNUAL REPORT

OF THE

TRUSTEES

OF THE

HOLTON LIBRARY,

BRIGHTON,

FEBRUARY 1st, 1866.

BOSTON:
CHARLES H. CROSBY, PRINTER,
Nos. 11 & 13 WATER STREET.
1866.

TOWN OF BRIGHTON.

HOLTON LIBRARY, Feb. 1, 1866.

To THE AUDITORS:

Gentlemen,—I have the honor to transmit to you, herewith, the Second Annual Report of the Trustees of the Holton Library, prepared in obedience to the Ordinance adopted by the Town, April 8, 1864.

Yours respectfully,

BELA S. FISKE,

Secretary of the Board of Trustees.

SECOND ANNUAL REPORT

OF THE

TRUSTEES OF THE HOLTON LIBRARY.

IN obedience to the Ordinance respecting the Holton Library, adopted by the Town of Brighton, April 8, 1864, the Trustees have the honor to submit their Second Annual

REPORT.

By the removal from town in October last of Mr. John Ruggles, the office of President of the Board of Trustees, which he held, was made vacant. The following communication is taken from the Records:—

TO THE SECRETARY OF THE TRUSTEES OF THE HOLTON LIBRARY:

Dear Sir,—I hereby respectfully submit the resignation of my office on the Board of Trustees of the Holton Library.

It is with regret that I am compelled to sever my official connection with gentlemen with whom my relations have been so pleasant, and for whom I entertain sentiments of sincere respect and personal regard. But I am happy to be assured that, under their wise guardianship, the Library will become what its founder intended it should be, an ever-increasing fount of light and knowledge.

Very respectfully yours,

JOHN RUGGLES.

BRIGHTON, June 12, 1865.

Mr. Ruggles, by request, retained his position until October.

In Board of Trustees, November 13, 1865, Mr. William Wirt Warren submitted the following Resolutions, which were adopted :—

Resolved, That we accept, with regret at its necessity, the resignation of Mr. Ruggles; and tender him our thanks for the interest he has taken in the Library, and for his exertions in its behalf.

Resolved, That we feel that in his removal from the town, this community has lost a valuable citizen; but we are happy, also, to be assured that, although absent himself, his influence will still be present, and his example will not be lost upon us.

Resolved, That a copy of the foregoing Resolutions be transmitted to Mr. Ruggles.

Mr. Ruggles, as Principal of the High School, some eighteen years, had been so closely identified with the educational interests of the town, as to render his co-operation on the Board of Trustees especially valuable. His associates, in their review of the year, cannot omit this renewed expression of their estimation of his services, and of their warmest wishes for his health and happiness.

The office of President was filled by election in the Board, November 13. At the same time, also, Mr. Edmund Rice was chosen to supply the existing vacancy on the Board of Trustees.

The Trustees would first direct the attention of their fellow-citizens to some alterations which have been made, the past year, in the rooms of the hall, much to the advantage of the Library. The portion of the first story of the Town Hall, originally granted for its use, embraced an uninterrupted area of about seventy feet by twenty, which was divided into two apartments by spacious folding doors between. The first apartment, opening on Washington Street, was designed for the general Reading Room, through which all visitors passed into the inner apartment, and to the Librarian's desk for the general delivery. This arrangement was found inconvenient, as materially interfering, by the entrance of visitors, with the stillness required for a reading-room. The desk has accordingly been removed from the inner to the outer apartment, directly in front of the folding doors. A small private door in the rear of the desk connects with the inner apartment, through which the Assistants pass in taking books to the desk, and in replacing those returned, thus obviating the necessity of continually opening the large folding doors, and rendering the inner apartment quiet. As those persons who come only to take or to return books do not enter at all into the inner apartment, it remains without interruption for all such as wish to sit and read. It is enjoined by the Rules and Regulations, that conversation and all unnecessary disturbance be avoided in this apartment; and the Trustees would recommend to all citizens who, complying with the regulations, have enrolled their names at the desk, and received Library cards, to use this room for its prescribed purpose,—either in perusing the various Reviews which are found upon the tables, or, by permission of the Librarian, in consulting the valuable collection of books of reference which may not be carried from the hall, or by reading such books designed for delivery as they wish.

Eight tiers of shelves around the walls have been already filled, those on the the north end of the hall being protected by glass doors. On the demand for more shelf-room, we have erected three alcoves, extending from the north wall, some eight feet into the room, open on either end, and with shelves on both sides, which will accommodate several thousand volumes more. A handsomely carved railing, in banister-finish, has been completed around the room, in front and within three feet of the shelves, enclosing also the alcoves, which railing, visitors do not pass. The excellent full-length portrait of Mr. James Holton, the founder, presented by Mr. Theodore Matchett, as described in the last Report, is hung in this apartment, as also the large engraving of the battle of Gettysburg, embracing nine square feet, which was presented by Mr. John Ruggles. The entire floor is protected from the reverberation of footsteps by neatly-fitted matting; and we believe few institutions of the kind offer rooms more commodious and attractive than these.

Mr. Winship of this town has served us another year as Librarian, with the lively interest which he has manifested in the institution from its commencement. His Report is herewith appended. Without robust health, and sharing, moreover, the arduous labors of the School Committee here, he has given gratuitously even more time, we feel, than we could justly claim, from his office duties in Boston. He was authorized to employ an assistant; and Mr. Webster Franklin Warren of this town, student of the Cambridge Law School the past two years, has been retained on a small salary. Other service has been regularly rendered by Zachary Taylor Cushman, and by William Henry Pierce, pupils of the High School.

Mr. Winship having declined serving as Secretary of the Board, to which office he was re-elected in March last, Mr. Bela Stoddard Fiske was chosen in his place.

A catalogue of the Library, which has been some time in preparation, will shortly be printed. As detailed in the last Report of the Trustees, the Brighton Library Association, incorporated January 15, 1858, was dissolved, and its books surrendered to the Holton Library, on the institution of the latter. This Association had, itself, received the books of a yet earlier library, the Brighton Social Library, namely, one of the earliest, indeed, of the kind established in the State, having been organized March 1, 1824.* The printed catalogues of the Brighton Library Association, with the names of the many new books procured from the Holton Fund, entered on blank leaves, have been thus far used by us, while the work of

---

* It is stated on good authority, that the first *Social Library* of common or popular books for popular use in our country, was probably that of the "Library Company," as it was called, in Philadelphia, founded at the suggestion of Dr. Franklin in 1731, by the young mechanics of that city, where he was then a young printer.

arranging the new catalogue has gone forward. These old catalogues, however, have been a serious embarrassment, and to most of the citizens who have failed to enter the new books in their copies, almost useless. The selection of books by visitors to the Library has, in consequence, been much hindered, and, in the judgment of the Librarian, the proportionate number of books taken out, the past year, has been somewhat lessened. We have been anxious to obtain as many new books as possible before printing the catalogue, else a supplement will too speedily be required. Although a complete catalogue cannot now be furnished but at much greater cost than in former years, the Trustees are assured alike in its absolute need, as well as in the general impatience of the applicants for books, that it should be no longer delayed.

The financial condition of the Library is presented in the Report of the Treasurer, Mr. Life Baldwin, which is herewith appended. It will be seen that on the funds loaned to the Town Treasurer the rate of interest has been increased from six per cent. to seven and three-tenths. Insurance has been effected on the Library for five years and on favorable terms with the Suffolk Insurance Company, Boston.

The whole number of books belonging to the Library, is three thousand five hundred and sixty-five. Of these, six hundred and sixty-two were added, the past year, by purchase, and seventy by donation. The names of the donors are given in the Librarian's Report; and letters of grateful acknowledgment on the part of the Trustees have been returned to them. We would particularly commend to the citizens this method of increasing the Library beyond the supply of books procured each year from the stated funds. The gift of but a single volume from each individual able to furnish the same, would materially increase the annual supply. We recollect the eloquent appeal of Edward Everett, President of the Board of Trustees of the Public Library, Boston, at the dedication of their building, to his fellow-citizens, to donate thus but a single volume each year to the collection. That some, at least, have heeded his suggestion, the annual list of donations since has testified; one thousand pamphlets, and nearly as many volumes, having been presented last year. The population of Boston is just about fifty times larger than our own population. A thousand volumes in her population would be as twenty in ours. Shall not a thousand volumes in donations to her library be answered by our proportionate supply of twenty volumes to ours? Our donations received in 1864, were far more than this, namely, seventy-three volumes and sixty-five pamphlets.

Of course much more variety will be secured to the Library, where eligible books, which individual tastes and preferences have selected, shall, after having been read by their owners, be transferred as gifts to the shelves. Each individual donor, too, must be gladdened in the thought that the volume which has entertained and profited him, or her, is now to go on a wider circuit, for further good. Nor is it out of place, in this connection, to renew the request, that individual tastes and preferences may be so far consulted, in regard to purchased books, as that all persons desiring certain books to be placed in the Library, will signify the same. A record-book, entitled "Books Asked For," is kept by the Librarian for the purpose; and in this, all persons are earnestly desired to enter the titles of such books as they wish added, with their own names, and that of the street on which they reside, attached.

The Trustees have endeavored, in the selection of books, to meet the reasonable expectations of all classes of readers. They have furnished, certainly, a good proportion of the lighter literature of the day; while the complete works of most of the standard writers of England and America, together with translations from the best foreign literature, and treatises, ancient and modern, in the various departments of science and art, have been added. They have aimed, in short, and will endeavor to gather here, all the most desirable books for general reading, as fast as issued from the press; and, as far as practicable, such works for special investigation and study as may be required.

Since the Library was first opened to the public, September 3, 1864, nine hundred and eighty persons have signed the promise to conform to the Rules and Regulations, and have received cards to take out books. The attendance at the rooms is somewhat larger in the evenings than in the day. The Institution is already established in popular favor, and waits but the wise counsels of those who shall hold it in trust, and the faithful use of its treasures by the citizens, to prove itself a vast benefit to the town.

The wise counsels of its Trustees, and the faithful use of its books and privileges by the citizens,—these remain the two essential conditions of its complete success. The founder of the Library, of whom a biographical sketch is contained in the last Report, devised generously and with a warm interest in the welfare of his native place, for the establishment of the Library. The town has very liberally seconded his bequests in handsome provision for its accommodation and maintenance. The Trustees promise their best endeavors to make the Institution what their retiring President has so happily expressed it, "An ever-increasing fount of light and knowledge." They trust, moreover, that their successors in office, as wider experience in the use of the Library shall develop new methods of administration, will be able to bring far wiser counsels than theirs to its government. Of the second essential condition above named, of the prosperity and success of the Library, the Trustees would now speak.

While the use of the Library by the citizens has been, in general, no otherwise than we could desire,—while the books have, for the most part, been earnestly sought and promptly returned and in good order, ordinary wear and tear, of course, to be always excepted, some individual cases of the abuse of books remain to be mentioned. The Librarian has called attention to this subject in presenting what he deems wilful injury in the soiling and mutilating of some of the books. We cannot urge too earnestly upon all who enjoy the privileges of the Library, the importance alike of care in the use of books and conformity to the Rules and Regulations, as also of coöperation in discovering by whom any wilful injury is done, that so, by such, the injury may be repaired.

With sorrow, with righteous indignation, may we not say, that such abuses as these seem inseparable from similar public Institutions which are generously opened for the happiness and improvement of all classes? Before referring to the Report of our own Librarian, our interest had been deeply engaged in the lately published Report, the thirteenth, of our neighbors, the Trustees of the Public Library of Boston, in which these same abuses, carried, as we read it, to an alarming extent, are detailed.

The President of the Boston Library writes thus :—

" At first the Trustees were led to hope that their success had been absolute ; that all had received and used the attractive privileges of the institution in the liberal and faithful spirit that had offered them. But, before long, it was found that a number of books were defaced by vulgar writing in them. Others were wilfully mutilated. A few disappeared. Still, the evil was so very small, and the benefits from the freest use of the Library were so great and so certain, that no change was deemed desirable. Everything was left as unrestricted as possible ; but everything was exactly reported to the City Government.

" In 1857, the evil had somewhat increased ; not much, indeed, but still so much that it began to be noticed more anxiously in the Annual Reports of the Trustees, where it has continued to appear ever since. Even the Reading Room, with its excellent collection of periodical literature and works of reference,—where everybody has been admitted with the least possible reckoning or reserve,— has, for the first time during the last year, become the subject of abuses too serious to be overpassed. Since the first of December last, forty-six numbers of different valuable journals have been stolen ; —many more have been mutilated by cutting out what was deemed useful or agreeable by the persons who so shamelessly abused the privileges they enjoyed ;—and a still greater number have been so wilfully defaced, that it is necessary to replace them by other copies. In the Library, there has been a corresponding unprecedented abuse. During the year ending August 1, four hundred and eighty-nine books disappeared, which it has not been possible to trace and recover; and many more were mutilated and otherwise wilfully and discreditably ill-treated. The Trustees make these statements with great regret and pain."—*Boston Report*, pp. 10, 11.

The Examining Committee of the Boston Library enlarge upon the same abuses in these terms :—

"They cannot forbear expressing their profound astonishment that there should be any persons in this community so lost to all respect for books, and so regardless of their own duties to this community, through whose liberality they are all enabled to take out and to use the books, that they can be guilty of wilfully injuring some of the most valuable works contained in the Library. Doubtless, many mark on the leaves, and do other injury, from thoughtlessness. This palliation cannot be extended to others, who are evidently gross culprits, and, as such, should be dealt with by the higher power of the law. It would be impossible to cite the numerous abuses of this kind; but two come up prominently before the Committee. A long addition sum, occupying the whole of the fly-leaf of a fine copy of 'Enoch Arden,' is a specimen of *thoughtlessness*. A gross attack upon the memory of our martyred President, written in doggerel lines, and surmounted by the late, so-called, Confederate States' flag, on the fly-leaf of another equally valuable work, is a specimen of the *wilful* injury of city property. Evidently, it has become the duty of some one to see that such desecration shall not be allowed hereafter. Otherwise, in addition to the injury which the Library will sustain, we shall encourage, not a sacred regard for books, but shall promote in the youth of this community a tendency to the desecration of them, than which scarcely anything could be more injurious in a Republic.

"As this is a general subject, and similar troubles will arise in other cities of the Commonwealth, the State should be appealed to; because, on occasions of gross misuse of the books, and in which the evidence seemed all-sufficient to convict, the City Solicitor declared the contrary to be the fact under the present law.

"The Committee would, therefore, respectfully, but earnestly, submit to the Trustees, whether the time has not fully come for them, as guardians of this city property, to give official notice to the city authorities that the Trustees cannot, under existing laws, properly defend what has been committed to them, and for asking that the city would appeal to the State for further legislation upon the subject.

" The undersigned would also suggest the propriety of having the books from a part of the Library carefully collated when taken, and when they are returned to the Library, whatever the expense that may be incurred in so doing, in order that, immediately upon any injury having been committed, the offender may be punished by a withdrawal of his right to take out books until the Trustees have acted upon the case. It may be a question whether a similar plan might not be pursued in this Library to that followed, at times, by the British Museum, viz.: whether the most grossly abused books should not be conspicuously placed to the public view? This method, whether thought wise or not by the Trustees, would be very effective in preventing similar offences being hereafter committed. Notices might also be posted on the backs of the books, requesting every citizen to aid in preventing injury to them, and informing offenders that they will be punished. If the State should pass any law, the legal penalty for abuse should be also thus placed on every book."

" All *unnecessary conversation* should be *interdicted*. One of the undersigned was in the hall for nearly an hour, and all the while a gentle ' *tete-a-tete* ' was being carried on by a young couple, who had found the luxurious chairs a pleasant spot in which to pass an agreeable hour."—*Boston Report*, pp. 24, 25, 26, 35.

The Superintendent of the Boston Library, Professor Charles C. Jewett, after alluding to missing books, thus writes :—

" In several instances, it is certain that no such person had ever resided in the houses designated upon their cards." * * * * " The principal loss and injury fall upon two classes of books—namely, novels and books for the young." * * * * "The injuries to books by marking and mutilation have (I mention it with much regret) noticeably increased. These damages, it should be remembered, are *cumulative;* so that, although the number reported each year may not seem very considerable, the aggregate, in a series of years, becomes a striking feature, and one by no means pleasing.

"The losses and injuries in the Reading Room have led to the adoption of important but indispensable changes in the conditions for the use of the periodicals." * * * * "They [these abuses] are *discreditable*, and, by the toleration of them, the Library fails so far, in one of its duties,—that of educating the public in their respect for books. The increase of the evil points surely to a day when a due regard for property held in trust for future as well as for present use, may demand a greater degree of stringency than has heretofore been thought imperative." * * * * "It is for them [the Trustees] to judge whether the time has, or has not come, to establish some stricter regulations than have heretofore been made, even should it be at the probable expense of a temporary decrease of the circulation and of some consequent dissatisfaction." — *Boston Report*, pages 44, 46.

These extracts are given in the hope that by a picture of abuses practised on a wide scale, even where ampler remedial measures are at hand than small towns can enjoy, our own citizens may better understand and more earnestly strive to abate the kindred abuses of which we complain.

Yes, these testimonies prove that everywhere, be it in town, or city, where blessed agencies are provided for the amelioration of the human condition,—always, where generous hearts devise benevolent Institutions for diffusing knowledge, for promoting human comfort, for staying the floods of ignorance and vice,— will be found the indifferent, the careless, the vicious, who will return their proffered advantages with foul abuse. Let not, therefore, liberal hearts be deterred from founding such Institutions, nor generous men and women, who would best serve their God in best serving their generation, withhold earnest coöperation. Let us not be weary in well-doing, for in due season we shall reap if we faint not, is a glorious Scripture exhortation and promise not less needed by us, to-day, than by the noble Paul who uttered it, under difficulties and discouragements ten-fold greater than ours, eighteen centuries ago.

No place so favored that wrong-doing, moral corruption, evil communications in school or college, vice in some of its forms shall enter not. The particular exciting causes which may exist more or less in one or another locality, are of little consequence so long as by them all the same sad result of sin is reached. We protest against the too common practice of charging on this or that place of residence the entire occasion of immoralities, of ruined characters and blasted hopes which simply a change of city, or town location should have prevented.

We heard a fond parent once say in Boston, in the hearing of children, "If only we could leave the city and bring up our children in the country, how happy should we be; for in Boston are they so exposed to temptations at every turn, to vice in its manifold forms,—to vicious companions and associations even in their schools, that I fear indeed for their safety." Said another parent, and again in the hearing of children, "Would that we could remove to the city, where, you know, their schools would be so much better, and they should be free from the temptations which beset them here in the streets." Equally mistaken and pernicious the utterances from both these parents! These remarks, in the presence of such eager young listeners, seemed to us little better than a license for vice. From such statements often uttered, be it in print or in conversation, what better impression can the young especially derive than that they must of course be vicious, unruly, mischievous, heedless of the right use and care of books, of teachers' counsels and educational privileges, because they happen to live amidst the peculiar temptations and vices of city or country, of a commercial, or a market, or an agricultural, or a manufacturing district!

No, beware lest unconsciously we educate the young in views

so false and fatal. Would we free our Public Libraries from the abuses complained of, whether in our largest cities, or in our smallest townships, let these abuses be met by the united, resolute determination of all to discover and bring to punishment their authors. Let the arm of the law be interposed. Let further State legislation be sought, if need be, as recommended in the Boston Report to cure the evils complained of there. Let all, in every place, earnest for human improvement, the diffusion of knowledge, the promotion of virtue and religion, help create a sound public sentiment, needed alike in town and city, that shall both discountenance and overpower these abuses.

Then shall our own Library do its best work in our community. The Trustees commend it confidently to the favor and use of the citizens. With good hope they commend it, notwithstanding such discouragements as they have felt bound to detail, and which attend kindred Institutions elsewhere. To the diffusion of knowledge among us they commend it; to the entertainment and instruction of the young and the old; to the establishment of correct principles in morals and philosophy; to the promotion of virtue and piety. They rely on it greatly to foster a correct literary taste, a love for reading and study in the young of both sexes, which shall lead them to seek the highest educational advantages within their reach. The Trustees believe that through the influence of the Library seconding the work of our public schools, our young men will more and more enjoy the advantages of our neighboring University. The names of six, in the different departments of the University, are entered in the last College Catalogue. The School Committee informed us in their Annual Report, 1861, that there were then a larger number of young men at the University from this town *in proportion to the population*, than from any other town or city in Middlesex County, not excepting Charlestown, Cambridge and Lowell. This estimate was at once seen by comparing the population of each town given in the census with the number of students from each on the catalogue. May the Library in the future help to plant early in the minds of our young people those seeds of knowledge which shall thus ripen into the fair fruits alike of moral and intellectual culture.

All which is respectfully submitted,

In behalf of the Trustees.

FREDERIC A. WHITNEY,

President.

WILLIAM WIRT WARREN,
JOSEPH ADAMS POND,
GRANVILLE FULLER,
JOHN PERKINS CUSHING WINSHIP, *Librarian.*

EDMUND RICE,
LIFE BALDWIN, *Treasurer.*
THEODORE MATCHETT,
BELA STODDARD FISKE, *Secretary.*

FREDERIC AUGUSTUS WHITNEY,
WEARE DOW BICKFORD,
JOHN PAINE CUSHMAN,
NATHANIEL JACKSON,
  Trustees by triennial, biennial and annual election.

HOLTON LIBRARY, January 31, 1866.

REPORT

OF THE

LIBRARIAN OF THE HOLTON LIBRARY.

To the Trustees:—

The Librarian herewith submits the second report for the year ending January 31, 1866.

The present condition of the Library is as follows:

Number of volumes belonging to the Library, exclusive of pamphlets, at the commencement of the year,		2,833
Number of books purchased—		
For circulation,	646	
For reference	16	
		662
Number of volumes presented		70
Total number of volumes February 1, 1866,		3,565
Number of subscribers,		452
" books taken out during the year,		12,658
" days the Library has been open,		93
Average number of books taken out per day,		136
Amount expended for books,		$1,092 34
" due for periodicals, 1864–5,		93 25

PERIODICALS.

Atlantic Monthly.	Genealogical Register.
Leslie's Magazine.	Scientific American.
Eclectic Magazine.	Harpers' Weekly.
U. S. Service Magazine.	Army and Navy Journal.
Cornhill Magazine.	Littell's Living Age.
Harpers' Magazine.	Punch.
Godey's Magazine.	The Horticulturist.
North American Review.	Our Young Folks' Magazine.

CATALOGUE.

The average number of books delivered each day has been somewhat smaller during the past than in the preceding year. This is to be attributed to the want of a complete catalogue. The old catalogues, in the copious supply of new books, have become of little account to their holders. The demand for the new catalogue is so urgent that the plan at first proposed of a somewhat elaborate work has been abandoned. We simply present the names of the books, with the names of the principal authors, duplicated.

In re-arranging the books in the Library, all works of reference, as also of poetry, history, biography, travels, fiction, &c., are assigned to separate places, the more readily to be referred to.

With the new catalogue in the possession of every signer, it is confidently believed that the number of books called for in the coming year, will be greater than ever.

INJURY TO BOOKS.

It is unpleasant to record the fact, that a number of books have been abused; the leaves torn out, or marked upon; the covers injured, and many returned much soiled.

True, those most injured are principally those most called for. Still, much of the injury is manifestly not ordinary wear and tear, but the result of most culpable carelessness; and, of course, as in cases of writing, of wilful abuse.

The By-Laws are perhaps sufficiently stringent to meet such cases when clearly known; but it is almost impossible, by reason of the number of signers to be waited on, to examine all books when returned, so as completely to identify the offenders. The Trustees of the Public Library, Boston, treat fully in their last Report of abuses precisely similar, and express strongly the need of more vigilant measures for detection, and even of extra State legislation. Perhaps we may find the needed remedy in the employment of an extra assistant, who shall attend exclusively to these cases, with a view to the enforcement of the By-Laws.

LITERARY EXERCISES.

The Librarian, in view of this valuable collection of books, cannot but express the hope that they may lead to the re-establishment of a society among the young men for literary exercises and debate. Hitherto such exercises have been conducted here with considerable interest and success; but the cost of hiring a hall, together with other expenses in sustaining such a society, have led to its discontinuance. Should the Trustees see fit to grant their hall under suitable restrictions and regulations for such exercises, it is believed that with the good number of books of reference, so needful in preparation for debate, our young men would again gladly avail themselves of the privilege of preparing and reading literary essays, and conducting discussions. A most valuable opportunity for improvement would be thus afforded them, a higher literary taste would be acquired, and the best books, rather than the lightest and most exciting, would be more and more sought by them.

A number of valuable Public Documents presented to the High School by Hon. William S. Damrell, have been transferred to the Library. They were rarely, if ever, consulted at the school, and were supposed to be of greater use for reference in the Library, where they are temporarily placed.

The fines collected during the past year, amounting to $62.68, are proportionately greater than before; and might be so modified as to fall more lightly upon those who have sufficient excuse for delay in returning books.

The Assistant Librarian, Mr. F. Webster P. Warren, has faithfully discharged the duties assigned to him, and with Z. T. Cushman, W. H. Pierce, and J. R. Brock, aided efficiently in forwarding the catalogue.

Appended is a list of donations made during the past year.

All of which is respectfully submitted.

J. P. C. WINSHIP, *Librarian*.

BENEFACTORS

TO THE

HOLTON LIBRARY,

For the Year 1865-66,

And the Number of Volumes, Pamphlets, Charts, &c., received from each.

James Holton's Original Bequest, . . $6,000.

Name.	Pamphlets.	Vols.
Boutwell, George S. Hon.	10	10
Boston Public Library, by Edward Capen,	15	–
Cushman, John P. Rev.	5	1
Matchett, Theodore	–	2
Mercantile Library Association, Boston,	1	–
Pond, Joseph A. Hon.	4	18
Sumner, Charles Hon.	–	6
Silloway, Thomas W. Rev.	1	1
Trustees of Brookline Library,	–	1
Whitney, Frederic A. Rev.	6	6
Winship, J. P. C.	50	24
Wheildon, William W., Charlestown,	–	1
	92	70

Second Report of L. BALDWIN, Treasurer of Holton Library, submitted February 13, 1866.

LIFE BALDWIN, AS TREASURER, in account with HOLTON LIBRARY.

DR.			CR.	
1865.			1865.	
Jan. 20.	For note against Town of Brighton	$5,000 00	May 25.	By cash paid Hooper, Lewis & Co., their bill $10 90
" 20.	" balance of cash on hand brought forward	11 45	June 16.	" J. P. C. Winship, for Nichols & Noyes' bill 269 90
" 30.	" cash of Librarian, for fines	5 36	" 27.	" J. P. C. Winship, his bill 17 55
March 23.	" " " "	5 00	Sept. 7.	" J. P. C. Winship, his bill 1 96
June 15.	" " " "	12 00	" 22.	" J. P. C. Winship, for p licy of ins ance on Library 60 00
July 12.	" cash of Town Treasurer, one year's interest on note	295 00	" 30.	" for check stamps 0 20
Sept. 7.	" cash of Librarian, for fines	13 96	" 30.	" J. P. C. Winship, for Nichols & Noyes' bill 104 08
1866.			1866.	
Jan. 16.	" " " "	19 40	Jan. 2.	" J. P. C. Winship, for Hooper, Lewis & Co.'s bill 26 00
" 23.	" cash of Town Treasurer, six months interest on note of $4,500 at the rate of six per cent. for two months, and 7 3-10 for four months	153 00	Feb. 12.	" J. P. C. Winship, for W. H. Piper & Co.'s bill 133 05
Feb. 13.	" cash of Town Treas'r, balance of the amount due from the Town for the year 1865, as provided by law	314 50	" 12.	" J. P. C. Winship, for Lovering & Co's bill 178 33
" 13.	" cash of Librarian, for fines	6 96	" 12.	" J. P. C. Winship, for Nichols & Noyes' bill 47 63
			" 10.	" J. P. C. Winship, for Nichols & Noyes' bill 152 69
			" 13.	" W. F. Warren, for W. H. Piper & Co.'s bill 23 65
			" 13.	" W. F. Warren, for Hooper, Lewis & C's bill 10 50
			" 13.	" W. F. W n, for J. P. C. Winship's bill 18 25
			" 13.	" W. F. Warren, for Nichols & Noyes' bill 65 08
			" 13.	" W. F. Warren, for Nichols & Noyes' bill 82 13
			" 13.	" W. F. W n, for J. P. C. Winship's bill 6 96
				By balance in hands of Treasurer, being of Note against the T n of Brighton for $4,500 and ash, $127.77. 4,627 77
		$5,836 63		$5,836 63

21

THIRD ANNUAL REPORT

OF THE

TRUSTEES

OF THE

HOLTON LIBRARY,

BRIGHTON,

FEBRUARY 1st, 1867.

BOSTON:
CHARLES H. CROSBY, PRINTER,
Nos. 13 & 46 WATER STREET.
1867.

THIRD ANNUAL REPORT

OF THE

TRUSTEES

OF THE

HOLTON LIBRARY,

BRIGHTON,

FEBRUARY 1st, 1867.

BOSTON:
CHARLES H. CROSBY, PRINTER,
Nos. 13 & 46 WATER STREET.
1867.

TOWN OF BRIGHTON.

HOLTON LIBRARY, Feb. 1, 1867.

To THE AUDITORS:

Gentlemen,—I have the honor to transmit to you, herewith, the Third Annual Report of the Trustees of the Holton Library, prepared in obedience to the Ordinance adopted by the Town, April 8, 1864.

Yours respectfully,
B. S. FISKE,
Secretary of the Board of Trustees.

TRUSTEES
Of the Library from its Commencement.

BALDWIN, LIFE	1864
BENYON, ABNER INGALLS	1866
BICKFORD, WEARE DOW	1864
CUSHMAN, JOHN PAINE	1864–66
FISKE, BELA STODDARD	1865
FULLER, GRANVILLE	1864
HUTCHINSON, CHARLES CARROLL	1864–65
JACKSON, NATHANIEL	1864
MATCHETT, THEODORE	1864
POND, JOSEPH ADAMS	1864
RICE, EDMUND	1865
RUGGLES, JOHN	1864–65
WARREN, WILLIAM WIRT	1864
WHITNEY, FREDERIC AUGUSTUS	1864
WINSHIP, JOHN PERKINS CUSHING	1864

OFFICERS
Of the Library from its Commencement.

PRESIDENTS.

JOHN RUGGLES,	April 18, 1864—October 9, 1865.
FREDERIC AUGUSTUS WHITNEY,	November 13, 1865—

SECRETARIES.

JOHN PERKINS CUSHING WINSHIP,	April 18, 1864—March 13, 1865.
BELA STODDARD FISKE,	March 13, 1865—

TREASURER.

LIFE BALDWIN,	May 23, 1864—

LIBRARIANS.

JOHN PERKINS CUSHING WINSHIP,	June 13, 1864—July 9, 1866.
WEBSTER FRANKLIN WARREN,	July 9, 1866—

THIRD ANNUAL REPORT

TRUSTEES OF THE HOLTON LIBRARY.

IN obedience to the Ordinance respecting the Holton Library, adopted by the Town of Brighton, April 8, 1864, the Trustees have the honor to submit their Third Annual

REPORT.

In the last Report, mention was made of the new Catalogue then in preparation. In order to complete the same, it was found necessary to call-in the books, and close the Library while they were re-numbered and re-arranged. This work occupied more time than was anticipated; and the general impatience of the citizens at being debarred the use of the Library several months, spoke well for their interest in the same. A handsomely-printed Catalogue, in octavo form, under the double arrangement of book-titles and authors, was at length furnished, and the Library was again opened to the public on the sixth of June last. Inasmuch, nevertheless, as the most complete Catalogues, so soon as printed, become straightway incomplete by reason of constant additions to the Library, so, already, must the Supplements on the tables be consulted, would one learn what books are weekly added to the collection.

On the ninth of July Mr. Winship resigned the office of Librarian; and Mr. Webster Franklin Warren, Assistant Librarian, was appointed his successor. The Trustees unanimously adopted the following Resolutions, expressing their appreciation of his services : —

Whereas, Mr. John Perkins Cushing Winship, who has most faithfully filled the office of Librarian of the Holton Library since its establishment in 1864, declining all pecuniary compensation, asks now to be relieved of the duties of the same,—Therefore,

Resolved, That the Board of Trustees present Mr. Winship their sincere thanks for his continued and devoted services.

Resolved, That we attribute the present prosperous condition of the Institution, in a great measure, to his excellent judgment in the office ; and that while we are still to have his counsels at our Board and on the Library Committee, we join with grateful acknowledgments of his past assistance, our warmest wishes for his health and happiness.

Resolved, That these Resolutions be entered on our Records ; and that the Secretary transmit a copy of the same to Mr. Winship.

On the tenth of September last, Mr. Abner Ingalls Benyon was elected a member of the Board of Trustees in place of Rev. John Paine Cushman, who had removed from town.

The citizens are referred to the Report herewith appended, of the Treasurer, Mr. Life Baldwin, for a statement of the financial condition of the Institution. It will be seen that the funds hitherto loaned to the town have been invested in United States Bonds, bearing interest, seven and three-tenths per cent.

In addition to the income of these funds, the town is authorized, by a recent Statute of the Commonwealth, to appropriate for the maintenance of its Public Library, a sum equal to half a dollar on each of its ratable polls. The number of ratable polls in this town is now somewhat more than one thousand; thus adding more than five hundred dollars annually to the Library Fund.

The Report of the Librarian, Mr. Warren, is likewise appended. From this it appears that the whole number of volumes belonging to the Library is four thousand and seventy-four. Of pamphlets unbound there are two hundred and thirty-seven. Of this collection five hundred and twenty-three volumes and forty-seven pamphlets were added the past year, of which four hundred and sixty-six volumes and twenty-seven pamphlets were purchased, and the remainder were given. Letters of grateful acknowledgment on the part of the Trustees have been returned by the Librarian to the donors, and their names will be found in his Report. All the numbers of reviews and periodicals received at the Reading-room have been bound, up to January, 1867, and the volumes placed with their sets on the shelves.

The Librarian has been authorized to employ a second assistant, that the labor of delivering and receiving the books might be facilitated. Hitherto it has not always been found convenient to deliver books immediately on their being returned by other borrowers, since opportunity was hardly afforded to replace them on the shelves, or to give them any examination. A second assistant is now charged specially with this service; and borrowers can usually receive the book sought, though it have but shortly before been brought-in to the desk. Zachary Taylor Cushman, and William Henry Pierce, have been employed as assistants to the Librarian.

The Trustees have considered from the beginning that the privileges of the Library were, both by the terms of Mr. Holton's Bequest and by their own commission from the town, to be confined to citizens and residents of the town. They have accordingly felt bound, in one or two instances, to refuse the use of the books to persons living beyond the limits of the town, as, for instance, in Brookline. In this they have followed the example of the Trustees of the Public Library of Boston, who, in repeated instances, have declined the use of that Institution to non-residents, even though large owners of real estate, and doing business in the city.

An application, however, was made to the Board, in October last, for extending the privileges of the Library, which seemed to a majority to constitute an exceptional case. It was presented by the commissioned officers stationed at the United States Arsenal in Watertown, on our northern border. It was urged in their communication that they were not really citizens of any town; that they were not voters anywhere; that their residence was strictly neither in town nor State, nor under local jurisdiction, but was the property of the United States; and further, that there was no Public Library in Watertown, nor in the adjacent town of Newton, or city of Cambridge, for whose privileges they could apply. A difference arising in the minds of the Trustees as to their duty in the case, the subject was under consideration at one or two meetings. The application was granted; the Third Article, Chapter Second, of Rules and Regulations for the use of the Library, having been amended. This Article read as follows:—

"Any resident in town, over the age of fourteen, may have the use of the Library upon signing a promise to obey its Rules and Regulations, and may take there-from one volume at a time."

And it was amended by the addition of the following clause, namely:—"*Provided*, That this Article shall not be understood as forbidding the use of the Library to Commissioned Officers of the United States, stationed at the Watertown Arsenal."

It may be added that members of the Board who were not quite satisfied of their right thus to extend the privileges of the Library beyond the town limits, felt also, that in this instance, some injustice might be done to residents at the Watertown Arsenal other than the Commissioned Officers, of whom, at some periods of the year, more than a thousand soldiers and other employees have been enumerated.

In connection with the above named alteration of the By-Laws, it may be well here to state all alterations which have been made since the organization of the Library.

Chapter I., Article 2, last clause, which read,—"At all meetings a majority of the Trustees shall constitute a quorum," is amended, and now reads, in place of "a majority," "five members."

Chapter I., Article 6, sixth clause, is amended by substituting " once a quarter," in place of " on or before the first day of February, annually."

Chapter II., Article 1, last clause, which read " No books, however, shall be delivered for two weeks immediately preceding the annual town meeting," is amended by substituting for " annual town meeting," " first day of February."

With the accessions made to the Library the past year, and with the prospect of constant valuable increase, the Trustees congratulate the town on its condition and usefulness. They took occasion in their last Report to describe particularly the Library Hall, with its accommodations for a Reading-room, likewise the Hall for the delivery and reception of books; and they are happy to report the general good order which has prevailed, the faithful manner in which the Librarian and his assistants have fulfilled their duties, and the present condition of the books. It appears that two books only are missing. One of these, under the title " Hugh Worthington," is not charged to any one, nor is it in its place. Any information respecting the stray volume will be gladly received at the Library. The other was carried away by a citizen who removed to Cambridge. On application made for it in form prescribed by the By-Laws, the borrower acknowledged its loss by him, and his purpose to restore its value. This, on repeated application, he has failed to do; and the Trustees have forborne to resort to legal measures for its recovery, trusting that as this delinquency is the first instance of the kind which has come to their knowledge, it may be the last. Each borrower, before enjoying the privileges of the Library, promises to obey the prescribed Rules and Regulations, by affixing to them his signature. The sixth and seventh of these, in Chapter II., are in words as follows: —

" Any book retained beyond the time prescribed by these Regulations shall be sent for by the Librarian; and the expense incurred in obtaining it shall be paid by the delinquent."

" All injuries to books beyond reasonable wear, and all losses, shall be made good to the satisfaction of the Board, by the persons liable; and any book not returned within one week after demand for it made by the Librarian, shall be regarded as lost."

The Librarian reports some instances of the defacement of books by writing upon and by tearing the leaves. It may be remembered that in their last Report, the Trustees brought this subject particularly to the attention of the citizens, and quoted from the Report of the Trustees of the Public Library of Boston, some cases of careless treatment and of intentional injury of books in that Institution, which had prompted suggestions for the remedy of such abuses. With the multiplication of public libraries in our towns and cities, the attention of the community is turned more to this matter of the abuse of books by some heedless or malicious ones who share the privileges of the same. We are happy to see that public sentiment has been so far awakened in Massachusetts to the importance of the subject, that in our Legislature, on the twelfth of January last, a Bill was introduced in the Senate, making it a penal offence to mutilate books belonging to a public library.

Of course, even with no malicious intent on the part of borrowers, books will experience very different treatment in care and handling from one and another reader. Nor can it be deemed unseasonable that as the authorized custodians of a precious charge, the property of the citizens, we entreat their co-operation in keeping unsoiled these fair-leaved messengers as they pass from household to household on their errand of truth, dispensing everywhere, we trust, some light, joy, comfort and peace. How sacred the office of a good book! What should be cared for if not this! How should children, especially, be both early and earnestly trained to the careful handling, the tender treatment, as well as the wise improvement of books! Shall counsels abound for the neat and tidy adornment of the person, and less care be bestowed on the orderly keeping of books? Shall fashion, with such exacting demands, regulate the costume of the body, and good sense, right principle, think less for the due care of the covers and leaves of a book? Quickeners of thought, food for the mind, without which it pines so hopelessly, nutriment for the undying soul, good books claim, surely, our best care,—nay, challenge, do they not, our best love? Indeed, Milton, in his Areopagitica, spoke not too strongly those memorable words: "As good almost kill a man as kill a good book; who kills a man, kills a reasonable creature, God's image; but he who destroys a good book, kills reason itself." * * * * "A good book is not absolutely a dead thing; the precious life-blood, rather, of a Master Spirit; a seasoned life of man embalmed and treasured up on purpose to a life after life."

The books most worn are found to be those of the lighter form of literature, as might be expected; as novels, travels, biographies and popular histories. Every public library that would satisfy the wants of a whole community, must provide a due proportion of these works. The complete works of the best and most noted writers of fiction, as Scott, Dickens, Cooper, Bulwer, Arthur, Marryat; Cervantes, in his forever famous work of Don Quixote; Mitchell, Thackeray, Hawthorne and Willis, Miss Edgeworth, Mrs. Stowe, the Warner's, Sisters, and Maria Cummins, who but recently, for us too soon, was called from earth, with their many compeers are on the shelves. With these are found, indeed, a host of lesser lights in the same department of literature, which, let us hope, do at least entertain, if not much instruct and improve, the many minds which crave them.

The proportion which works of fiction should bear to the entire contents of a public library, cannot easily be defined. In the Boston Public Library, as we learn from the recent Report, there are in the Lower Hall, which is chiefly frequented by borrowers as containing the popular books oftenest wanted, about twenty-four thousand volumes. Of these, about six thousand, one-fourth part, are novels, "of which," it is stated, "a larger use is made than of the other classes of books." We cite the language of the same Report commenting on the use thus made of the lighter form of literature, as applicable to our own case. "It is in many respects fortunate that the wear and tear of the Library falls mainly upon the class of works of the smallest relative importance among its possessions, and which can generally be so readily replaced when worn out, or lost."

On the other hand, the Holton Library offers to its patrons a large proportion of such works as probably will not soon be worn and defaced by use. On a brief glance at its catalogues, the names of authors flit before us, whose works we could wish might be handled more and more. We promise not to rebuke even a considerable honest rubbing of the recent sterling edition of the works of Lord Bacon, in three volumes crown octavo; the handsome volumes, in similar size, of the works of the Right Honorable Edmund Burke, ablest of statesmen, orators, writers,—whose title meant what it said; of Dugald Stewart, of whom it is well affirmed that had he lived in ancient times, his memory would have descended to us as that of one of the finest of the old eloquent sages;—the Academic Questions of Cicero, also his life in three volumes by Middleton, and, more recent, his life in two volumes by Forsyth, bringing Rome before us with the freshness of reality and the interest of the best romance. The lives of the Cæsars,—the immortal productions of Demosthenes and Plato, the Idyls of Theocritus, Bion and Moschus,—the lives and works of Herodotus, Thucydides and Xenophon, all, too, elegantly translated into your own tongue,— of Hannibal, Alexander, and Peter the Great, of William the Conqueror, the Charleses, the Philips, and Frederic the Great; the three authors who so well bring Cromwell before us, and the seven authors who, in twenty volumes, treat exhaustively of Napoleon, stand on our shelves. The half-score of authors, who, in their travels and explorations, have laid open for us in part the mighty continents of Asia and Africa, especially entertaining us by their travels in Central Asia and Africa,— or told us of Egypt and the Nile; the thirteen volumes from nearly half as many authors who treat of China and of Palestine; the Arctic Explorations, and Cruise for the Polar Sea, by Franklin, Hall, Hayes, and Kane;—the eleven volumes which furnish us the Cosmos and travels of Humboldt, are here.

The Library offers many works on the aborigines of this continent, and on the Indian races. The grand histories of Prescott and Sparks, of Bancroft, Palfrey, Motley and of Kirke in his Charles the Bold, must attract the old and young. The works of Fisher Ames, most accomplished orator, statesman, and political writer,—of the classic Irving, Channing, Dewey, Felton, Sumner, Hillard, Phillips, and of Winthrop, who, in the two elegant volumes, the last just from the press, of the life and letters of John Winthrop, has brought back to us, with the freshness of that earlier age, his renowned ancestor, the first Governor of Massachusetts, must not be passed by. The "Precious Thoughts" and seven other volumes of the gifted Ruskin, fond devotee of Art, require no recommendation at our hand. Memoirs of the beloved Fenelon, of Whitfield, of Judson, the saintly Baptist missionary, and of his gifted wife, "Fanny Forester," rise to view. The complete works of Tacitus the Roman, fitly described as "the most dignified of historians," who, born scarce twenty years after Christ, has incidentally verified in his writings the New Testament narratives, claim the perusal of all readers. Inviting editions of Josephus, the distinguished Jewish annalist, of Plutarch, Gibbon, Hallam, Lamartine, Mackintosh, and the brilliant Macaulay; the lives and works of Franklin, of General Warren, the Adamses, and Jefferson; of Webster, Calhoun, and Benton; of Story, Everett, and Choate; of Patrick Henry, Otis, and the Quinceys; and of Horace Mann, great educator of the people; the popular sketches of Bayard Taylor, of Lossing, Parton, Goodrich, Holland, Sargent, the Headleys and the Abbots; the scores of interesting and instructive volumes enumerated under the titles America, and American, Europe, and European, England, and English, France, and French, the United States, Italy, Rome, and the Roman Empire, Russia, Germany and Spain; the varied gifts of De Quincey and Victor Hugo; the quaint genius of Carlyle and Emerson; the quiet humor of Hood, the sparkling wit of Douglas Jerrold; the rare genius of Hawthorne, the entertaining pages of Thoreau, the sweetness of Charles

Lamb, in life and works, present themselves to our notice. Agassiz, Hitchcock, Silliman, and Hugh Miller, speak from the shelves. The best dramatists, led by Shakespeare,—poets of all ages, from Homer, Virgil, Horace, Ovid, Juvenal, each in fitting dress for our own tongue, with the treasures of Gœthe and Schiller, to the splendid modern editions of British and American poets,—with the letters of Beethoven, master of singers and musical composers, and of Mozart, whom, beyond his wondrous musical gifts, for his immortal requiem, alone, all should know, are here.

As still we turn the leaves of the catalogues, we meet standard treatises on Law and Jurisprudence, on Metaphysics, Natural History, and Philosophy, including Ferguson's large and valuable volumes, with a volume of plates; on Astronomy and Physical Science; on Political Economy, Anatomy, and Physiology; on Geography, Geology, and Chemistry; on Agriculture, and the Culture of Fruit; on Floriculture, Botany, and the Culture of Grapes. In the three latter departments, as likewise in the department of Natural Philosophy, we are happy to enumerate the names of three of our own citizens as authors,—Breck, Strong, and William Warren. Ecclesiastical History and the Reformation invite their readers; and Theology, including the recent great work of Sprague, in itself a small library, portraying the pulpits of the leading denominations of the Protestant Church in eight ponderous volumes which blend with varied instruction concerning learned men and their times, an infinite fund of anecdote and entertainment. Nor are sermons wanting here for the eyes of those whose ears take not in enough, of. which, a few among the many, are those of Channing and the Beechers, of Blair, Wayland, Dewey, King, Chapin and Spurgeon; of Parker, and of Swedenborg done in philosophy; of Lowell, Judd, and Harrington; of Porteus, Sterne, Strong, Smith, and Taggart; of Griffin and Pond; of Edwards, Kirk, and Stone; of Robertson, in Brighton, England; of the Peabodys and the Wares.

There are Essays learned as well as light, historical, biographical, critical and miscellaneous. Slavery, Temperance,

War and Peace, all are treated. A very full list of authors who have written of the life and character, of the time and services of Washington, is presented, and of those, also numerous, who have written of the martyred Lincoln, both fathers, indeed, of their country. Lafayette, and the Presidents of our nation,—the leaders, the origin and issues of the American Revolution may be studied here, and treatise on treatise concerning the late war is found here,—tribute on tribute to our brave soldiers and sailors, the living and the departed, with lives of Scott and Grant, of Sherman, Sheridan, Farragut, Butler, McClellan,—of the Jacksons, from Andrew, the never-guided, to poor Stonewall, the misguided; and of the Johnsons, with and without the *h*, from sturdy Sam and Ben, of English literature,—names familiarly so called,—to Andrew, of our own time and notice and circle.

Our Library is already enriched with the recorded lives and works of many gifted and saintly women. Though we rapidly glance at the catalogues, the names are seen of Madame de Stael, of Maria Edgeworth, of Lucy Aiken, of Hannah More, of Hannah Adams, Mrs. Hemans, Mrs. Opie, and Hannah Gould; of Mrs. Somerville, Mrs. Jameson, Mrs. Sigourney, and the Sedgwicks; of Mrs. Kirkland, Grace Greenwood, Mrs. Stowe, and Mrs. Child; of Lady Holland, Frederica Bremer, Mary Howitt, and Florence Nightingale; of Mrs. Browning, Frances Ann Kemble, and Margaret Fuller Ossoli; of Mrs. John Foster, Mrs. Follen, and Mrs. Farrar; of Mrs. Norton, the two Mrs. Ware, and Mrs. Mann; of Mrs. Hale and Mrs. Hall; of Eliza B. Lee and the Davidsons, Sisters; of Mrs. Howe and Mrs. Whitney; of Mrs. Charles and Mrs. Pike; of the Misses Porter, Alcott, and Dodge. Well-known names of female writers of fiction, and in the other departments of literature, still abound,—as of Southworth, Hofland, Evans, and Kavanagh;—of Hentz, Gaskell, Wood, and Grey; of Oliphant, Holmes, Thomas, and Gore; of Austen, Buckminster, Lander, and Forbes; of James, Richie, Radcliffe, and Strickland; of Stephens, the Brontés, Sanford, Yonge; and of some half hundred more whose various gifts are contributing to the instruction and entertainment of readers.

Many valuable volumes, denoted in the catalogues by an asterisk, are books of reference to be consulted and read in the Reading-room. Among these, Dictionaries, Cyclopædias, Atlases, Reviews, and Magazines hold an important place. The second volume of Allibone's great Dictionary of English Literature and British and American authors, of which the first volume, issued in 1858, is in the Library, will shortly be added from the press.

The Library, though in its humble beginning, thus presents considerable variety. Here it would seem might be found the different kinds of food enumerated by Lord Bacon, when, in speaking of books, he said so aptly, "Some are to be tasted, others to be swallowed, and some few to be chewed and digested." One danger of the popular library, doubtless, lies in this,—that it induces too much tasting and swallowing, and allows too little chewing and digesting. Checks and regulations for reading, however, are generally about as much heeded as when prescribed for eating and drinking. The over-sanguine Mentor is perhaps brought up in the midst of his good advice by the pointed utterance of Dr. Johnson, who writes so bluntly, "Read in a book when and where you are interested, and what interests you, and not otherwise." The judicious reader, nevertheless, must desire so to blend the great purposes of reading,—recreation and instruction, namely,—pleasure and profit, entertainment and improvement, that they may combine in the largest and noblest culture of the mind and heart.

For this great end our Library freely offers its treasures to the citizens. We need not remind them of the privilege which the generous founder of the Institution, seconded by their own ready and liberal action, has thus placed in their hands. The increase in the number of books taken out, the past year, as shown by the Librarian's Report, testifies to their appreciation of the same. Their gratified attendance on the course of able lectures given during the season just closed, under the auspices of the Returned Soldiers' Club, alternately at the Town Hall, and at Union Hall on Union Square, is but another expression of the same interest which we would foster more and more in the Library. Books and popular lectures as instruments in the diffusion of knowledge and of public instruction, so kindred are they, that we cannot forbear to put on record here, the course to which allusion is made.

It was opened at the Town Hall, Thursday Evening, October 4, by the Hon. George Sewall Boutwell, of Groton, on " Faith Essential to Success," and was continued by the Hon. George Stillman Hillard, of Boston, on " Books, their Use, their Selection,"—by Edwin Percy Whipple, of Boston, on " Shoddy," — by the Rev. Warren Handel Cudworth, of East Boston, late Chaplain of the 1st Massachusetts Regiment, on " Purpose," — by the Rev. William Rounsville Alger, of Boston, on " Chivalry,"— by the Rev. Jacob Merrill Manning, of Boston, late Chaplain of the 43d Massachusetts Regiment, on " Samuel Adams,"—by the Rev. Willard F. Mallalieu, of Boston, on " The American Idea," — by Benjamin Preston Shillaber, of Boston, on " Funn,"— by the Rev. Samuel Walton McDaniel, of Brighton, on " Physical Culture," — by the Rev. George Hughes Hepworth, of Boston, on " The Ideal Republic," — by George William Curtis, of New York, on " Conservatism,"—by the Rev. Edward Everett Hale, of Boston, on " The Northern Invasions." And the next lecture is announced to be given by our townsman and associate on the Board, Hon. Mr. Pond, President of the Massachusetts Senate.

Indeed popular lectures from distinguished men appear to have found favor for the last twenty years with our citizens generally. Courses of such lectures continued through the winter seasons, have been well sustained. We have before us the record of such lectures, with the names of their authors, extending back twenty years, until interrupted in 1862 by the excitements of the civil war. It is interesting to see how many of the eminent men of our time have been heard by our citizens, season after season, in these lectures. The lists have been printed each year, in the Reports of the School Committee, of which, complete sets, since the Reports were first printed in 1840, may be found in the Library.

The Public Library, the Public Lectures and the Public Schools, let them engage more and more the warmest interest of our people. Their benefits are mutually shared, each with the others. It is gratifying to learn from the last Report just issued of the Secretary of the Massachusetts Board of Education, that our Town stands fourth among the three hundred and thirty-five cities and towns of the Commonwealth, in its liberal support of her public schools; and that among the fifty-two cities and towns of Middlesex County she stands the first. It may be remembered that in this regard, in 1842 and 1843, she stood first in the Commonwealth two successive years. May equal liberality characterize the Town in the maintenance of its Public Library. We trust that the list of its benefactors may be each year lengthened. Most we desire that the number be increased of those, of whom now we know many, who wisely and faithfully improve its advantages. Sad the homes where good books come not at all! No longer is there any apology for one such home in our midst. Unfortunate the homes where showy furniture and costly adornings are held of more account than good books. In the list of authors enumerated above, a portion only of those included on the shelves, are many concerning whom we might well apply the familiar direction of Horace, in his Art of Poetry, respecting the Grecian Authors, —

"Nocturna versate manu, versate diurna."

Handle them day and night.

Leisure hours of the long summer days, and more, the long nights of winter, invite all to the perusal and the study of good books. The Trustees renew the request that individuals would at any time communicate through the record-book at the Librarian's desk, the names of books desired which they may not have procured. The grave as well as the lighter books must have place here. Some books that deserve, will not at once attract most readers. But we must remember, in selecting, the quaint saying of Thomas Fuller, whom, next to Shakespeare, Coleridge calls the most marvellous of writers, "Learning hath gained most by those books by which printers have lost." Nevertheless, for the wants of many minds let provision be made, so it be within the bounds of pure morals and correct taste.

For the young starting in the race of life,—for those in its active cares and duties,—for those " Past Meridian,"—for those " Looking Towards Sunset,"—for those in health and gladness, and those in sickness, sorrow, bereavement, — for the heart in all its varying moods, the gay and the grave, from careless childhood to the hour when shadows cast from the invisible world are gathering over it,—shall provision be made. For all, here wait the productions of the wisest and the best. Works made immortal by genius, sanctified by piety and learning, consecrated by noblest thought, by generous affection, by purest taste, wait here to enrich the mind. Voices from the past and the present call. " Doth not wisdom cry, and understanding put forth her voice? Unto you, O men, I call; and my voice is to the sons of man. Receive mine instruction and not silver; and knowledge rather than choice gold. For wisdom is better than rubies; and all the things that may be desired are not to be compared to it. Whoso findeth me findeth life, and shall obtain favor of the Lord."

All which is respectfully submitted,

In behalf of the Trustees.

FREDERIC A. WHITNEY,
President.

FREDERIC AUGUSTUS WHITNEY,
WEARE DOW BICKFORD,
ABNER INGALLS BENYON,
NATHANIEL JACKSON.

WILLIAM WIRT WARREN,
JOSEPH ADAMS POND,
GRANVILLE FULLER,
JOHN PERKINS CUSHING WINSHIP.

EDMUND RICE,
LIFE BALDWIN, *Treasurer.*
THEODORE MATCHETT,
BELA STODDARD FISKE, *Secretary.*

Trustees by triennial, biennial and annual election

HOLTON LIBRARY, January 31, 1867.

REPORT

OF THE

LIBRARIAN OF THE HOLTON LIBRARY.

To the Trustees:

The Librarian herewith submits the third Report for the year ending January 31, 1867.

The Library is at present in the following condition:—

Number of volumes belonging to the Library at the commencement of the year	3,565
Number of volumes added by purchase, and by binding periodicals, including a few books accidentally omitted in last year's report	466
Number of volumes presented	57
	4,088
Number of volumes purchased to supply the places of volumes worn out or defaced	14
Total number of volumes February 1, 1867	4,074
Number of pamphlets, February 1, 1867	237
Number of subscribers for the past year	224
Number of subscribers since the opening of the Library in 1864	1,102
Number of subscribers who have taken out books during the year	686
Average number of books taken out by each subscriber	16
Number of books taken out since the re-opening of the Library in June	11,064
Number of days on which the Library has been open	63
Average number of books taken out per day	176
Amount expended for books and periodicals	$1,447 02
Amount received from fines	47 38

PERIODICALS.

Atlantic Monthly.
Army and Navy Journal.
Cornhill Magazine.
Eclectic Magazine.
Godey's Magazine.
Harper's Magazine.
Harper's Weekly.
Leslie's Magazine.

Littell's Living Age.
North American Review.
Our Young Folks' Magazine.
Punch.
Scientific American.
The Horticulturist.
U. S. Service Magazine.

At the time of the presentation of the Librarian's Report for 1865, the Library was closed for the purpose of completing the catalogue. So great was the demand for a new catalogue, that it was thought necessary to attend exclusively to that object, and no other work was attempted for the first four months of the year. The volumes, which had previously been placed on the shelves in the order in which they were purchased, were classified,—books relating to the same general subject-matter being collected together. Particular attention was given to obtaining complete sets of the works of the more prominent authors. The catalogue was completed and presented to subscribers about the first of June, when the Library was re-opened, since which time nearly four hundred copies have been distributed to the various families in the town,—the rules of the Library allowing one catalogue to each family. The benefit derived by subscribers from the new catalogue is shown by the fact of the large increase in the number of books taken from the Library during the past year, over that of the previous year. The average number delivered per day during the last year, was nearly one-third greater than during the former year, so that the number of books loaned from the Library for the eight months in which books have been delivered this last year, is not very much less than the number loaned for the whole of the previous year.

With a few exceptions, the books have been promptly returned. After a thorough examination, your Librarian is able to report a loss of but two books since the opening of the Library in June last. Of one of these books, the title of which is "Hugh Worthington," nothing is known. Perhaps it may yet be found if all who have read it will take the trouble to ascertain whether they have returned it to the Library. The other was properly delivered to Mr. Thomas W. Dempster, and by some accident destroyed while in his possession. Mr. Dempster has repeatedly promised to furnish a copy of the book so lost, but has never done so; and as he has now removed from the town, the prospect of ever receiving anything from him is very small. With the above exceptions, it is believed that all the volumes belonging to the Library can be accounted for.

The complaint, found in nearly all reports, of the careless use of books, is applicable to our own Library. Several of the works of the more popular authors are defaced by writing, and in a few instances the leaves have been torn out. This occurs most frequently in the books read by boys; as, for instance, the books of "Oliver Optic." Nearly all the works of this author are injured in some way, either by the loss of one or two leaves, or by writing, expressive of the reader's opinion of the book. It is hoped that parents will assist in correcting this fault, by showing their children the impropriety, to use no stronger term, of such proceedings.

An extra assistant has been employed for the last part of the year, whose particular occupation is to replace all books upon the shelves as soon as returned. By our former method, books which were returned to the Library on the evening of one day, were not available to subscribers until the next Library day, so that many of the books most frequently called for, although in the Library, could not be assorted and delivered. Some dissatisfaction was caused on this account; but by the new arrangement, all reason for complaint is removed, and every facility is given to readers to procure any book which is in the Library at the time of their application.

The latest copies of all the magazines enumerated in our list of periodicals, may always be found on the tables of the Reading-room; and the "Galaxy," "Genealogical Register," and "Every Saturday," are to be added to those already mentioned. A large number of works on various subjects, too valuable for general circulation, may be there consulted by subscribers upon application to the Librarian.

In accordance with the By-Laws, the Library was closed for the two weeks immediately preceding the first of February, for the purpose of making the annual examination. Many of the subscribers object to having the Library closed at this time, on the ground that they are thus deprived of reading-matter at the time when they have most leisure. The subject is here brought before your notice, that you may take such action, if any, as seems advisable.

Appended is a list of donations made during the past year.

All of which is respectfully submitted.

W F. WARREN, *Librarian.*

BENEFACTORS

TO THE

HOLTON LIBRARY,

For the Year 1866-67,

And the Number of Volumes, Pamphlets, Charts, &c., received from each.

James Holton's Original Bequest . . . $6,000.

Names and Residence.	Pamphlets.	Vols.
Boutwell, George S. Hon., Washington, D. C.	14	10
Boston Public Library	1	—
Braman, Chandler B., Brighton	—	5
Breck, Joseph, Hon., Brighton	—	1
Brighton, Town of	—	2
Mason, Augustus, Dr., Brighton	1	—
Pond, Joseph A. Hon., Brighton	2	8
Pratt, Isaac, Brighton	—	1
Rice, Edmund, Brighton	1	
Sumner, Charles, Hon., Washington, D. C.		
Strong, William C., Brighton	—	1
Waltham, Public Library of	—	2
Warren, William, Brighton	—	4
Whiting, William, Roxbury	—	1
Whitney, Frederic A. Rev., Brighton	—	17
Whitney, Mrs. Frederic A., Brighton	—	1
Wilson, Henry, Hon., Washington, D. C.	—	3
	20	57

Winship, J. P. C., Brighton, six Maps.

Third Report of L. BALDWIN, Treasurer of Holton Library, submitted February 14, 1867.

LIFE BALDWIN, as Treasurer, in account with HOLTON LIBRARY.

Dr.

1866.			
Feb. 13.	For note against Town of Brighton	$4,500	00
" 13.	" balance of cash brought forward	127	77
" 15.	" cash of W. F. Warren, refunded to cent error	10	50
July 11.	" cash of H. H. Larnard, Mr, Town appr'n		
	priation in part	450	00
" 11,	" cash of H. H. Larnard, Treasurer, six months'		
	Inst on note	162	00
Oct. 17.	" cash of H. H. Larnard, Mr, interest on n to		
	to date	77	50
Nov. 14.	" cash of H. H. Larnard, Town appropriation for		
	1866, balance due	99	00
" 19.	" ash of Mian, for fines as per memorandum	27	79
1867.			
Jan. 15.	" cash for six months' interest on $3,800, 7 3-10 bonds	138	70
Feb. 12.	" cash of Librarian for fines. (See Memorandum)	19	59
		$5,612	85

Cr.

1866.			
April 27.	By cash paid J. P. C. Winship, for W. V. Spencer's bill	$32	75
" 27.	" J.P.C. Winship, for Crosby & Ains nh's		
	bill	95	23
	" Rev. F. A. Whitney, for bill of sundries	7	90
	" W. H. Piper, for bill of b ks	75	00
	" Chas. H. Crosby, for printing catalogues	356	00
	" Hooper, Lewis & Co., for paper, &c.	23	50
June 12.	" Nichols & Co's, for b ks	142	15
July 12.	" Nichols & Co's, for books	262	79
" 12.	" W. F. Warren, for stationery	4	10
" 18.	" Johnson & Co., for Atlas	17	50
" 18.	" Rev. F. A. Why, for Spencer's bill	11	06
" 20,	" Nichols & Noyes, for b ks	74	45
Oct. 10.	" Hooper & Lewis, for seals	6	00
" 10.	" premium on $3,800 7 3-10 bnds, 5 7-8		
" 18.	" used Inst on 7 3-10 94 lys	223	25
Nov. 19.	" Baker & Iden, for mps	71	44
" 19.	" Librarian, for bill of sundries	7	00
Dec. 5.	" 1 Im, for J. Vanderslice's bill	12	85
" 5.	" Pit, for W. S. Pit's bill	4	50
" 12.	" Librarian, for J. P. C. Winship's bill	7	67
" 12.	" J. H. Simps n, for b k	4	00
" 12.	" Charles H. Crosby, for catalogues	3	00
1867.		18	50
Jan. 7.	" Nichols & Noyes, for books	83	76
" 7.	" for check stamps	0	20
Feb. 7.	" Nichols & Noyes, for books	48	72
" 7.	" Charles H. Crosby, for labels	3	00
" 8.	" Crosby & Ainsworth, periodicals, 2 years	137	27
" 12.	" W. S. Bartlett, for book	3	33
" 12.	" Librarian, for sundries	4	99
		$1,741	91
" 14.	Balance in hands of Treasurer, consisting of $3,800 in 7 3-10 U. S. bonds, and cash, $70.94	3,870	94
		$5,612	85

FOURTH ANNUAL REPORT

OF THE

TRUSTEES

OF THE

HOLTON LIBRARY

BRIGHTON,

FEBRUARY 1st, 1868.

BOSTON:
ROCKWELL & ROLLINS, PRINTERS,
122 WASHINGTON STREET.
1868.

FOURTH ANNUAL REPORT

OF THE

TRUSTEES

OF THE

HOLTON LIBRARY

BRIGHTON,

FEBRUARY 1st, 1868.

BOSTON:
ROCKWELL AND ROLLINS, PRINTERS,
122 WASHINGTON STREET.
1867.

TOWN OF BRIGHTON.

HOLTON LIBRARY, Feb 1, 1868.

TO THE AUDITORS:

Gentlemen,—I have the honor to transmit to you, herewith, the Fourth Annual Report of the Trustees of the Holton Library, prepared in obedience to the Ordinance adopted by the Town, April 8, 1864.

Yours respectfully,

B. S. FISKE,
Secretary of the Board of Trustees.

TRUSTEES
Of the Library from its Commencement.

BALDWIN, LIFE	1864
BENYON, ABNER INGALLS	1866
BICKFORD, WEARE DOW	1864
BRECK, CHARLES HENRY BASS	1867
CUSHMAN, JOHN PAINE	1864–66
FISKE, BELA STODDARD	1865
FULLER, GRANVILLE	1864
HUTCHINSON, CHARLES CARROLL	1864–65
JACKSON, NATHANIEL	1864
MATCHETT, THEODORE	1864–67
MATCHETT, WILLIAM FREDERIC	1867
POND, JOSEPH ADAMS	1864–67
RICE, EDMUND	1865
RUGGLES, JOHN	1864–65
WARREN, WILLIAM WIRT	1864
WHITNEY, FREDERIC AUGUSTUS	1864
WINSHIP, JOHN PERKINS CUSHING	1864

OFFICERS
Of the Library from its Commencement.

PRESIDENTS.

JOHN RUGGLES,	April 18, 1864—October 9, 1865.
FREDERIC AUGUSTUS WHITNEY,	November 13, 1865—

SECRETARIES.

JOHN PERKINS CUSHING WINSHIP,	April 18, 1864—March 13, 1865.
BELA STODDARD FISKE,	March 13, 1865.

TREASURER.

LIFE BALDWIN,	May 23, 1864—

LIBRARIANS.

JOHN PERKINS CUSHING WINSHIP,	June 13, 1864—July 9, 1866.
WEBSTER FRANKLIN WARREN,	July 9, 1866—

FOURTH ANNUAL REPORT

OF THE

TRUSTEES OF THE HOLTON LIBRARY.

IN obedience to the Ordinance respecting the Holton Library, adopted by the Town of Brighton April 8, 1864, the Trustees have the honor to submit their Fourth Annual

REPORT.

Two vacancies on the Board of Trustees were filled by the Town at the annual meeting in March last. The first was occasioned by the removal from Town of Mr. Theodore Matchett, one of the original members, who from the commencement of the Library had devoted himself most faithfully to its interests, and who had been one of its most generous benefactors. Mr. William Frederic Matchett was elected in his place.

The other vacancy was created by the resignation of Hon. Joseph Adams Pond, likewise an original member of the Board, and at the time President of the Massachusetts Senate. In a letter from the Senate Chamber, under date of February 8, 1867, addressed to the President of the Board, he asks to lay down this trust; pleading his numerous official and commercial labors as hindering the discharge of his duties to the Library. As our last Report was passing through the press, we had opportunity only to announce that the closing lecture in the course with which, through the winter, we had been favored by some of the ablest lecturers in the country, all whose names, and subjects of discourse were thus far detailed in the Report, would be given by Mr. Pond. He accordingly lectured at the Town Hall, on the evening of the 13th of March last, taking for his subject, "Fortune in War." The theme was exceedingly well treated, it is perhaps needless to add; and, with Mr. Pond's excellent address, was made highly effective. Who of us could have imagined that his familiar voice would never again, thus publicly, be heard among us?

On Thursday morning, 24th October last, he left his home here, as usual, for the city. Calling at the State House, then undergoing repairs and alterations, and for superintending which work, he was one of the State Commissioners, he was seized with apoplexy, borne unconscious into the capitol, and thence to his father's house in Boston, where, on Monday, the 28th following, he expired, coming not again to his home among us, and was interred with public honors at Mount Auburn on the 31st. Well had it been for his sorely bereaved family, for the church to which he was devoted, for the community and the commonwealth whose good he so faithfully sought, had he sooner laid down, and more, the trusts which the growing regards of the people confided to him. An overtasked brain thus ended, at the early age of forty, the earthly life of one whose course from boyhood had been stamped with integrity, the vigor and maturity of whose powers were so lovingly consecrated to the service of God and man. Most fitly and gladly we record here this brief tribute to our late colleague and fellow-citizen, who, himself a frequent donor to the Library, brought to our counsels the valuable experience which had been acquired in other and in similar relations; and whose short life, so filled with labors well discharged and with promise for years to come, verifies anew the grand old Scripture, that "Honorable age is not that which standeth in length of time, nor that is measured by number of years; but wisdom is the gray hair unto men, and an unspotted life is old age."

The seat at our Board thus vacated by Mr. Pond, whose elected term had not expired, was filled by the appointment of Mr. Charles Henry Bass Breck.

The election of officers took place, agreeably to the By-Laws, at the first meeting of the Trustees after the annual Town meeting. The officers of the past year were re-elected.

The citizens may be gratified that the time for closing the

Library for its annual examination has been changed from February to August. The former month, with its long evenings and comparative leisure, is more favorable for reading than the latter with its heat; and many had expressed their unwillingness to be deprived of the books at a season when they could most enjoy them. The public schools, moreover, are closed in August, and many persons, old and young, are absent from their homes. At the Boston Public Library, as at first organized, the same inconvenience was experienced; and, but a few years since, by a change in the ordinance, the month of August was substituted for the time of the annual examination. Our last report enumerated all the alterations, which had then been made in the printed Rules and Regulations as distributed among the citizens. Accordingly we put on record here the recent alteration by which the Library will not be closed until August next.

Chapter II. Article 1, last clause, which read "No books, however, shall be delivered for two weeks immediately preceding the first of February," is amended by substituting for "first of February" "fifteenth day of August."

Chapter II. Article 2, first clause, which read "All books shall be returned to the Library on or before the first day of February," is amended by substituting for "first day of February" "fifteenth day of August."

The Report of the Treasurer, Mr. Life Baldwin, which is herewith appended, will exhibit the condition of our finances. The Town, at the last annual meeting, generously authorized the Trustees to draw on the Treasury for one thousand dollars, should that sum be desired, in addition to the interest of the invested funds, for the maintenance of the Library. The citizens have indicated by this vote that they were not willing to forego the advantage of keeping the Library supplied with the new books desirable in such an institution, as they issue from the press.

The accompanying Report of the Librarian, Mr. Warren, states that the whole number of volumes belonging on the 1st February, 1868, to the Library, which is yet but in its infancy, is four thousand four hundred and twenty-one! Of pamphlets unbound there are six hundred and eighty-nine. One hundred and nineteen volumes and thirty-four pamphlets were presented to the Library the past year.

By the 6th Article, Chapter I., of the Rules and Regulations, the Librarian is required to record, in a book kept for that purpose, the name of every donor to the Library; the property given; the date of the donation; the estimated value thereof, and the conditions, if any, on which given; and shall likewise return in printed certificate form, to each donor, an acknowledgment of thanks on behalf of the Trustees.

It will not be deemed invidious if, among the donors of the past year, all whose names are appended to the Librarian's Report, we particularly refer to the largest donor, the first President of our Board, Mr. John Ruggles, for eighteen years the successful Principal of the High School in this Town, and at present a resident of Brookline. In addition to previous benefactions, he has now presented fifty-four very desirable volumes, all handsomely bound, the current value of which, as appraised in the Record, is not less than one hundred and twenty-five dollars. Among these is a set of Harper's New Monthly Magazine, in thirty-five volumes, complete to the present year, — volumes which, with their numerous and beautiful illustrations, are as popular with the readers of the Library as they are instructive and useful. In the note accompanying the donation, Mr. Ruggles kindly expresses his best wishes for the continued success of the Library, and for the health and happiness of its officers.

The usual acknowledgment of the Trustees has been already tendered to Mr. Ruggles. But they gladly avail themselves of this renewed opportunity to reciprocate the friendly sentiments he has communicated, and to convey more publicly the assurance of their sincere sympathy with him in his recent domestic bereavements, and their unabated regards for one so long their esteemed fellow-citizen and attached associate in public and private relations.

We state with pleasure that more books have been presented during the past than in any previous year. Our Senator, Hon. Charles Sumner, and our Representative, Hon. George Sewall Boutwell, have continued their valuable donations of Congressional and other Public Documents, bestowed every year since the founding of the institution. And a lady, Mrs. Tyler, some years since removed from Town, has remembered her native place in a donation to its Library. Still, the number of donors among our own citizens, embracing now a population of nearly five thousand, has been very small. How considerable might be the increase in this way would the many individuals among us, abundantly able, contribute but a single volume each year! Would that the same liberality might be displayed towards our Library by its own patrons and friends as has been bestowed on the Boston Public Library. We learn from the last Report of the Trustees of that Institution that " Nearly one half of the collection of books, and a vast preponderance — say all but about two thousand pamphlets— have been the gift of three thousand two hundred and seventy-nine persons and institutions, not enumerating anonymous donors, and counting the same source each time that it appears on the annual return of donors. This one half is independent of the purchases with the interest of the trust funds, which are in fact, likewise, the fruit of private munificence. If we add these to the casual presentations, it would show that the vast majority of our books is the result of other causes than the city appropriations. The average yearly number of casual donors has been about two hundred and nineteen; and the past year there were three hundred."

In the same valuable Report a comparison is instituted between the number of donations made to the Boston Public Library and to great libraries elsewhere. The Manchester Free Library, that of the British Museum, four of the chief free libraries of England established under the Public Library Acts, the Library of Harvard University, the Astor Library, of New York, the Library of the Boston Athenæum, the New York Mercantile Library, are contrasted, in respect to the extent and value of donations, with the Boston Public Library, and the result is largely in favor of the latter. Indeed, from the Boston Report of 1852, ten years after the establishment of the Library, and five years after the dedication of the present fine structure on Boylston Street, it appears that more than three quarters of the books, then numbering one hundred and five thousand and thirty-four, had been presented to the city.

To these interesting annual Reports of the Trustees of the Boston Public Library, of which the complete series from the establishment of the Library in 1852 to the present year stands on our shelves, and all of which, until his death in 1865, were from the pen of its first and gifted President, the late Edward Everett, the attention of the friends of our Library is commended.

Is not this generous spirit in such a cause, to which, through these citations, we have referred, worthy of emulation? How easily might one thousand individuals in this Town present, next year, that number of volumes to our shelves in addition to those which shall be purchased. Among the names of donors enrolled on our Librarian's present Report, is that of an esteemed widow, a mother in our Israel, who has nearly reached her eightieth year, offering two good volumes ; the " widow's mite," as modestly she styles it. One of these volumes may be found of special interest to many of our older native citizens, as coming from the pen of a gifted authoress whom they have known here formerly, Mrs. Harriet V. Cheney, the daughter of Rev. John Foster, D. D., for more than forty years pastor here, — pastor of the undivided Town.

Liberality of the kind thus commended, which seeks to enlarge and prosper a free Public Library, where the poor as well as the rich may be supplied with good books, seems to us to bear a very kingly stamp. Very much it seems to us as that " quality of mercy " of which Shakespeare has told from the lips of his noble Portia, which

> "Is not strained;
> It droppeth as the gentle rain from heaven
> Upon the place beneath. It is twice blessed;
> It blesseth him that gives, and him that takes."

Whosoever gives a good book to be read which, without the giving, might not so have been read, is himself richer in the deed. "There is that scattereth and yet increaseth." Let us suppose that Solomon when he wrote these words, about one thousand years before Christ, looked through the ages of barbarism that were to roll over the earth, before Christian civilization and general knowledge should establish Public Libraries for the people, and would enforce by them the very generosity which we here urge, to-day. At any rate, it were well to try his " scattering," of which he speaks in the proverb, and trust in the promise for the " increase."

Since the issue of the Catalogue in June, 1866, many books have been purchased, the titles of which are contained on the Supplements in manuscript at the Library. It is proposed to print, on some additional sheets, the names of the books thus far added. These octavo sheets, conforming in size with the Catalogues, will be of great service to all who use the Library; and may be laid within the covers of the Catalogues already in their hands.

These additions comprise many of the most desirable books for popular use which have been published in these two years past, as well as many of earlier date. All works in series, which were in the Library at its opening, have been kept complete; as the Annual Cyclopædia, the continuation of the New American Cyclopædia, now comprised in twenty-two volumes, royal octavo,—the various Magazines, Journals, Reviews, which, as they come out in parts, are laid upon the tables of the Reading Room, and regularly bound. Valuable works in history, as Motley's United Netherlands, volumes third and fourth; Bancroft's History of the United States, volume ninth; the second volume of Life and Letters of Governor John Winthrop, by his descendant, Hon. Robert C. Winthrop, announced in our last Report as just issuing from the press; the second volume of Napoleon's Julius Cæsar, and second volume of Greeley's American Conflict; the second volume of the late lamented President Felton's Ancient and Modern Greece; Abbott's second volume of the Civil War in America; Essays and Reviews, with Lectures on Literature and Life, three volumes by Edwin Percy Whipple, first of American essayists; the wonderfully attractive historical novels of Louisa Mühlbach, some half score volumes; the admirable work of Upham, on Witchcraft, in two volumes, have been brought in.

Of the works of Francis Parkman we have added the last, the Jesuits in North America, having previously his History of the Conspiracy of Pontiac, Prairie and Rocky Mountain Life, Pioneers of France, and, in a somewhat different department, his fine treatise on Roses and their Culture. We shall greet the next volume from this gifted young author, already promised, as relating to the discovery and occupation of the valley of the Mississippi. To Thackeray's twenty-five volumes on our shelves, we have added one; to Mayne Reid's twenty-five, two; to Ik Marvel's eleven, which have charmed so many persons, three; to Marryatt's nineteen, two; to Oliver Optic's sixteen, eight; to J. S. C. Abbott's nine, one, namely, Lives of the Presidents; to J. T. Headley's nine, one. And these latter authors all, how popular have they proved with the young! The useful and entertaining works of Mrs. Pike (Anna Athern), and of Horatio Alger, which we had complete, are now continued. J. G. Holland (Timothy Titcomb), adds the touching poem "Kathrina," dedicated as the work of his hand to "Elizabeth, the wife of his heart," to the nine volumes already on the shelves from his pen. J. H. Gilmore (E. Kirke), adds three volumes to his eight; E. M. Sewell one to eighteen; the popular novelist, Arthur, one to twenty-three; Bayard Taylor, one to seventeen; Augusta Evans (Geo. Eliot), two to five; Mrs. Child, tender and brave in dealing with human wrong, with her Romance of the Republic; the gentle Grace Greenwood, with her Record of Five Years; and Gail Hamilton, of not the gentlest pen, with her Wool Gathering, her Red Letter Days, and her Woman's Wrongs, food so spicy as to increase the malady of all literary dyspeptics; Anna C. Ritchie, Mrs. Holmes, Mrs. Hall, with Carleton, Cutler in his stirring war lyrics, Samuel Osgood in his American Leaves, and William R. Alger with his great work on Immortality, his Genius of Solitude, and Friendships of Women, Holmes with his Guardian Angel, Emerson with his May-Day, Whittier with his Tent on the Beach, — all these supplement complete sets of their works already in the Library at the date of the Catalogue.

To the nine volumes of Charles Lamb, including his life by Talfourd, we have added Barry Cornwall's Memoirs of this sweet poet; to the eight volumes of Ruskin, his Time and Tide; to the Poems of Milton, his Prose Works; to the first volume of the Addresses and Speeches of Hon. Robert C. Winthrop, the second; to the numerous works on the late civil war, Kettell's History of the Rebellion, Frank Moore's Women of the War, Boynton's History of the Navy during the Rebellion, and many others; to Macaulay's brilliant History and Essays, in six volumes, his Speeches and Poems, in two more. Martineau, Guizot, Robert Collier, in his widely circulated Nature and Life; William Dwight Whitney, Professor at Yale, the American Orientalist, in his critical work on Language and the Study of it; the Life of Percival, the late American Poet and Scholar, whose merit was only equalled by his modesty; Griswold's Republican Court, with its admirable portraits of distinguished women; the Life of Madame Recamier, and the Life and Letters of Madame Swetchine; Ozanan's History of Civilization in the fifth century, in two volumes; Queen Victoria's early years of Prince Albert, and her Journey in the Highlands, just from the press; Beethoven's Letters, in two volumes; Kirkwood's able Treatise on Meteoric Astronomy; Homes without Hands, by the Rev. J. G. Wood; Dr. Hayes' Open Polar Sea, in addition to all which we possessed on Arctic explorations; Field's History of the Atlantic Telegraph, in addition to the works of Briggs, and of Prescott on the Electric and Atlantic Telegraph,—now enrich the Library.

Still following the line of the Supplement we meet with a book of which, perhaps, the title alone will ensure readers, — How to Make Money and How to Keep it. Anxious seekers shall at once be referred to its number, 4,074. Or, failing in this world-tried experiment, one can lay his hand resignedly on another book, A Thousand a Year; — or, if still Fortune says, not quite so fast as that, then take up a third book which is near, only a hundred and thirty-seven numbers beyond, Comfort for small Incomes, by Mrs. Warren, 4,211. Have not your Trustees sought to meet in their selection all possible emergencies? For those who would further investigate that awful delusion, if not sum of iniquity, Mormonism, we have added to works already on hand, the Mormon Prophet, by Wade, and Origin of Mormonism, by Tucker. For domestic economists, anxious how best to get heat, we have put in Peat and its Uses, by Johnson, and Facts about Peat, by Leavitt. Gardening for Profit is an excellent book for the opening spring, as is also the New Treatise on Beet-root Sugar, by Grant; Pomology of America, by Warder, in its thorough discourse and copious illustrations of fruit, almost tempts us to put the leaves to our lips, with the discourse in our minds. Darby's Botany of the South, Ornithology of New England, by Samuels, with elegant illustrations, and Rosevelt's Game-birds of America, demand careful handling in return for the delight they will afford.

So must that grand work of which the country may be proud, lately added to the Library, a Journal in Brazil, illustrated, by Professor and Mrs. Louis Agassiz. With the treatise on Brazil, by Kidder and Fletcher, and that by Ewbank, already in the Library, we have added, also, the late treatise of Codman; thus laying before our readers no inconsiderable information respecting that country so rich in its native resources and important in its relations to North America as to win more and more the regards of the United States.

In addition to the various Cyclopædias on hand, we have subscribed for the large work now in course of publication, the Cyclopædia of Biblical, Theological, and Ecclesiastical Knowledge, to be issued in five or six volumes, royal octavo, at a cost of thirty dollars. Some of the volumes are received, and will be found of special value to Sabbath School Teachers and Students of the Bible of all denominations. Professor Stowe's learned treatise on the books of the Bible is also received. The several Ecces, which, as meteors, have lately flashed brightly in the literary heavens, as Ecce Homo, Ecce Deus, Ecce Cœlum,—up, we fancy, as rockets, down much like sticks,—are waiting on the shelves for other readers. The Three Gardens, and Thanksgiving, recent volumes by Rev. William Adams, D. D., of Brooklyn, N. Y., formerly pastor of the second church in this town, will be especially interesting to his friends here.

The most reliable works on modern Spiritualism, selected by persons interested, have been supplied, including a large volume of Messages purporting to have come from John Quincy Adams in the spiritual world, to Josiah Brigham of Quincy, who has since followed his illustrious friend and townsman. Lest some faithless ones might discredit the genuineness and authenticity of these Messages, a volume of Letters known to have been written by this eminent man while actually in the body and on earth, has also been put in. Many additions have been made to the books which relate to England, Old and New, to Russia, France, Italy, Rome. The Worcester Association and its Antecedents, by Rev. Joseph Allen, D. D., just from the press, brings before us, with sketches of some modern divines, a body also of the distinguished clergymen of a former generation, with portraits of several in the antique clerical costume. To some twenty volumes upon the shelves on the American Revolution is now added Moore's Diary of the Revolution, and Goodrich's Signers of the Declaration; and to the many volumes on America, Martin Van Buren's Political Parties of America. The eventful Life of Major General Nathaniel Greene, of Revolutionary memory, lately published, offers a rich treat. The Army of the Potomac, Burnside and the Ninth Army Corps, and Richmond during the War, are added. Sheridan in Lee's Last Campaign comes, the complement of two other volumes, which we had, Headley's and Moore's lives of that eminent General. And the Life of Gen. Robert Lee, by McCabe, has been put in to assist in closing the verdict which posterity must pass on this able General, but, as Rebel Chieftain, most sadly misguided man.

We must not fail to commend, as among the gems of the Library, the interesting volume just sent from the press by a loving hand, the Life and Letters of Wilder Dwight, of Brookline. He was one of the noblest of the martyr-band in the late war. Among the first scholars of the class of 1853 at Cambridge, Major of the Second Mass. Volunteers in the second month of the war, and Lieutenant Colonel in one year after, he became first in all soldierly qualities, and fell at Antietam, September, 1862, in the vigor of his youth, leaving the record of a manly, Christian character which, as faithfully portrayed in these pages, no young man, it would seem, could peruse without profit. The Memoirs of Geo. N. Briggs, Massachusetts' upright Governor, instructive, engaging, true as he was true, must not be passed by. The Life of Benjamin Silliman, by Fisher, eminent among America's Sons of Science, and as Professor, the pride of Yale; the Memoirs of the distinguished President Wayland of Brown University, by F. and H. L. Wayland; and the Life of Josiah Quincy, of Massachusetts, illustrious statesman, loyal patriot, Christian patriarch,—have all been lately procured, and require no " words of brightening fame" to stamp them as works of rarest merit, because illuminated with a wondrous light reflected from their subjects.

Nor less renowned is yet another life which, recorded in most inviting form, is entered on our Supplement, and with which we close this hasty sketch of a few books among the many which are not named on the Catalogues in the hands of the citizens. We refer to the Life of Timothy Pickering, by his son, Octavius Pickering, to be issued in several octavo volumes, of which the first is received. He died as the last generation was leaving the stage. In a few touches his portrait may be sketched, which ampler materials in the fond and filial hand will complete. Born at Salem, in 1745, he died there in 1829, reaching almost fourscore years and four. Of stately, majestic presence, his manners were the index of his mind. A graduate of Cambridge in 1763, he was scholar, lawyer, counsellor, judge. The confidence of his townsmen was manifested in entrusting to him most of their municipal offices. As soldier, he was private, colonel, adjutant-general. He was member of the Continental Board of War in 1777, as, subsequently, in the war of 1812, he was a member of the Massachusetts Board of War. He was among the first to foresee the coming storm of revolution, and among the bravest to bide its coming. While yet it had not broken out, Gage, the Provincial Governor, caused the arrest of him and his colleagues on the Committee of Correspondence, for summoning a meeting of his fellow-citizens of Salem, to consider the sad state of affairs. But so odious was this act with the people, that the magistrate who had issued the warrant, was forced to recall it. Col. Pickering was the friend of Washington, under whose administration he served successively as Postmaster-general, Secretary of War, and Secretary of State. He was present at the siege of Yorktown, in 1781, and at the surrender of Cornwallis, as he had been with Washington at the battles of Brandywine and Germantown. Valiant in war, he was peacemaker with the hostile tribes of Indians, after sitting in the Convention to place on more stable foundations the great State of Pennsylvania through her revised Constitution. When the martial strife was over, he found delight, as Cincinnatus the Roman hero, and as Washington, in agricultural pursuits, and served as President of the Agricultural Society of his county. Successively member of the House of Representatives and senator in Congress, his large heart embraced all service. Religion in its loveliest form crowned and consecrated the character, where integrity, justice, benevolence, and the love of truth reigned from childhood. Noble type of character for building up and defending the State! Happy the age that brings in elegantly printed form such models before the public! Fortunate the towns that amidst the load of taxation incident to the war-burdened country, and amidst the rush of material interests, provide from the shelves of their Public Libraries such reading, not less for the rising than for the risen generation! Will not Young America turn more and more away from the light and frivolous literature that floods the land, to inform themselves of the master-minds of earlier and later time, as in specimens above enumerated?

So we have increased, and shall aim still to fill the Library with the best books that the press affords. The Report of the Librarian presents a favorable condition for the past year. In regard to losses, or injuries sustained, of which, in the Boston and other Public Libraries so much complaint has been hitherto made, and to which, special attention has been called in our own reports, he now gives us little to regret. The Librarian suggests some extension of the privileges of the Reading Room to children under the age of fourteen years. The third Article of Chapter II., Rules and Regulations, reads thus: "Any resident in town, over the age of fourteen, may have the use of the Library, upon signing a promise to obey its Rules and Regulations, and may take therefrom one volume at a time."

The use of the Library is thus free to every citizen over the age of fourteen, who has signed the Rules and Regulations. The Board will take into consideration the further extension of this privilege, as set forth by the Librarian. It will be understood that he uses the term subscribers in the sense of signers, only, — no pecuniary subscription being required, as in the case of some public libraries, for the use of this. From the number of volumes delivered, and from the general punctuality and care in their return, and from the interest manifested by those who read and consult the books and the various reviews and periodicals on the tables of the Reading Room, encouragement is drawn for the growing usefulness of the institution.

In our last Report allusion was made to legislative action, in the session of 1867, for providing redress in case of wilful injury to books. In Boston, where so much harm had been caused in this way in former years, those in charge complained that no means of redress were open for them in the courts. The legislative action above named resulted in the adoption by the General Court, March 16, 1867, of the following "Act for the Preservation of Books and other Property belonging to Public Libraries." "Whoever wilfully and maliciously writes upon, injures, defaces, tears, or destroys any book, plate, picture, engraving, or statue belonging to any law, town, city, or other public library, shall be punished by a fine of not less than five dollars, nor more than one thousand dollars for every such offence."

Thanking our rulers for their timely interference to meet and prevent wrongs that, as already committed, may be committed again, we add only, our assured trust that no occasion shall arise with us for calling upon their statute. We, in these pages, help only to spread it abroad. It was not in our time, nor as custodian of a public library, that the brave Paul uttered those words which eighteen hundred years have not put out of sight: " Rulers are not a terror to good works, but to the evil. Wilt thou then not be afraid of the power? Do that which is good and thou shalt have praise of the same."

The assistants named in the last Report were employed, during the early part of the year, in the service of the Librarian. As they both left town, Frederic Augustus Pierce and Hiram Norton Cushman, advanced pupils in the High School were engaged, and are still discharging their duties acceptably.

Each year records the establishment of free public libraries in other towns and cities of the Commonwealth. The Secretary of the Massachusetts Board of Education, in his annual report, 1867, presents in tabular form, statistics furnished him from fifty such institutions in this State. Only two of these were established before the Boston Public Library in 1852, which now numbers one hundred and thirty-six thousand (136,000) volumes. Our own Library dates from 1864. Brookline and Arlington on our borders have already such. Cambridge has no absolutely free library, but a small public library open to subscribers on payment of one dollar a year. The last annual college catalogue, it may be stated, in passing, enumerates as the total number of books in the various departments of the University, one hundred and seventy-six thousand (176,000), the largest collection on this continent. Newton, on our southern border, has recently taken action towards establishing a free library; and Watertown, more lately, at a town meeting on the 28th of last month, voted with great unanimity, to establish such a library, accepting the sum of six thousand dollars raised by subscription among the citizens for starting the same, and appointing a committee on its organization, of which Rev. John Weiss was chosen chairman. More and more may these beneficent institutions be multiplied.

It remains for us, in conclusion, once more to commend to our fellow-citizens the Library with whose management they have entrusted us, with much satisfaction in its past success and with good hopes for its future. They have not mistaken the wants of the time in following out the design of its generous founder, and appropriating liberally for its support. Educate the public taste by encouraging the love of reading among the people, and provide liberally for the various wants of many minds; and books shall be a match not alone for ignorance and error, but for much immorality and impiety that so love to keep them company. We confess to great reliance on good books to secure to willing and faithful readers all the benefits which were assigned them by the old poet. It was Denham, one of the fathers of English poetry, who wrote under Charles I., and under Cromwell and the Commonwealth, and whose dust has slept just two hundred years beneath Westminster Abbey, who penned the couplet so terse and true, —

"Books should to one of these four ends conduce,
For wisdom, piety, delight, or use."

Not to one of these four ends only, say we, but to all. In no way better may the efficacy of books hereto be tried, than through the popular free public libraries of our land.

All which is respectfully submitted,
In behalf of the Trustees,
FREDERIC A. WHITNEY,
President.

EDMUND RICE,
LIFE BALDWIN, *Treasurer*,
WILLIAM FREDERIC MATCHETT,
BELA STODDARD FISKE, *Secretary.*

FREDERIC AUGUSTUS WHITNEY,
WEARE DOW BICKFORD,
ABNER INGALS BENYON,
NATHANIEL JACKSON.

WILLIAM WIRT WARREN,
CHARLES HENRY BASS BRECK,
GRANVILLE FULLER,
JOHN PERKINS CUSHING WINSHIP.

Trustees by triennial, biennial, and annual election.

HOLTON LIBRARY, January 31, 1868.

REPORT

OF THE

LIBRARIAN OF THE HOLTON LIBRARY.

To the Trustees:

The Librarian herewith submits the fourth annual Report for the year ending January 31st, 1868.

The Library is at present in the following condition :—

Number of volumes belonging to the Library at the commencement of the year	4,074
Number of volumes added by purchase, and by binding periodicals and pamphlets	237
Number of volumes presented	119
	4430
Number of volumes purchased to supply the places of books worn out or defaced	9
Total number of volumes February 1, 1868	4,421
Number of pamphlets February 1, 1867	237
" added by purchase	419
" " " presentation	33
Total number of pamphlets February 1, 1868,	689
Number of subscribers for the past year	247
" since the opening of the Library in 1864	1,349
" of subscribers who have taken out books during the year	889
Average number taken by each subscriber	21
Number of books taken out during the year	18,590
" " days on which the Library has been open	102
Average number taken out per day	182
Amount expended for books and periodicals	$434 17
" received from fines	$65 00

PERIODICALS.

Atlantic Monthly.	Harper's Weekly.
Cornhill Magazine.	Leslie's Magazine.
Eclectic Magazine.	Littell's Living Age.
Every Saturday.	North American Review.
Galaxy.	Our Young Folks' Magazine.
Genealogical Register.	Punch.
Godey's Magazine.	Scientific American.
Harper's Magazine.	The Horticulturist.

The interest in the Library continues unabated, the number of books given out and the number of new subscribers being somewhat larger than last year. There is very little room for complaint in regard to the use of books loaned; the number found on examination to be so worn and injured as to be unfit for circulation being very small. In all such cases, duplicate books have been purchased to supply the places of those so destroyed; and the small number purchased during the year — only nine having been procured to supply such vacancies — attests the care generally manifested by those borrowing books.

From the best examination which can be made at present, the time for the annual examination having been changed from February to August, it appears that three books are lost, of two of which, "Ela; Delusions of the Heart," and "Charles O'Malley," nothing is known. The third, "Count of Monte Cristo," was taken by a party who has moved from town, and we have been unable to find either the subscriber or the book.

Such publications as have been considered advantageous to the Library, both of a transient and permanent nature, have been added during the year. The number of books presented is much larger than that of 1866, the donation from Mr. Ruggles, consisting in part of a complete set of "Harper's New Monthly Magazine," being nearly equal to the whole number presented during the previous year. Various other donations have been received, as shown by the list of donors appended.

Since the publication of the Catalogue, in June, 1866, about four hundred volumes have been added to the Library by purchase and presentation. As we have issued no Supplement, there is no way for subscribers to ascertain what new books have been added, except by the imperfect aid of a few catalogues at the Library in which all new volumes are entered. The number of books added does not, perhaps, yet call for a permanent Supplement; but a sufficiently accurate list can be printed with little expense; and if done, will be of great advantage to those who seldom visit the Library, but depend on the catalogues originally distributed.

The question, as to how far duplicates should be purchased, is still an open one. The demand for the works of the more popular authors of fiction is such, that unless there is more than one copy of the latest novels in the Library, many subscribers are obliged to wait, in some cases for months, before they are able to procure them. There is the objection that, as many novels are comparatively old after they have been published a year, and the demand for them has ceased, a large number of duplicates only serve to cumber the shelves and occupy the space that is needed for other volumes. The only books of which more than one copy has been purchased during the past year are the historical novels of "L. Muhlbach," for which the demand has been and continues to be very great.

As the By-Laws now read, only subscribers are allowed to consult books in the Reading Room. Applications have frequently been made by school children, under the prescribed age of fourteen, for permission to consult some of our books of reference in preparing their compositions. These applications have generally been allowed, although the children so applying were not subscribers, and so were not entitled to the use of such books. If the Regulations of the Reading Room can be so amended as to allow such persons under fourteen years of age, as will take proper care of books to which they may wish to refer, the use of the Reading Room, perhaps the efficiency of this branch of the Library would be increased. The magazines alluded to in the Report of last year, as "to be added," have been procured; and the list of magazines at present to be found on the tables of the Reading Room is included in this report. Back numbers of magazines may be consulted by subscribers on application to the Librarian.

Appended is a list of donations for the past year.

All of which is respectfully submitted,

W. F. WARREN, *Librarian.*

BENEFACTORS

TO THE

HOLTON LIBRARY,

FOR THE YEAR 1867-68,

And the Number of Volumes and Pamphlets received from each.

JAMES HOLTON'S ORIGINAL BEQUEST . . . . $6,000.

Names and Residents.	Pamphlets.	Vols.
Boston Public Library, Trustees of	1	—
Boutwell, Geo. S. Hon., Washington, D. C.	23	47
Dana Library, Cambridge, Trustees of	—	1
Peabody Institute, Danvers, Trustees of	1	—
Rice, Abigail, Mrs. Brighton	—	2
Rice, Edmund, Brighton	4	3
Ruggles, John, Brookline	—	52
Sumner, Charles, Hon., Washington, D. C.	—	8
Tyler, John S. Mrs., Boston	1	1
Waltham, Directors of Public Library of	2	
Whitney, Frederic A. Rev., Brighton	1	1
Whitney, Frederic A. Mrs., Brighton	—	1
Winship, J. P. C., Brighton	—	3
Worcester, Directors of Public Library of	1	—
	34	119

Fourth Report of L. BALDWIN, Treasurer of Holton Library, submitted February 14, 1868.

LIFE BALDWIN, as Treasurer, in account with HOLTON LIBRARY.

Dr.

1867.		
Feb. 14.	For bal. on hand, U. S. bonds $3,800, cash $70.94,	$3,870 94
May 15.	" cash of Librarian for fines, 3 mos. ending May 1,	12 57
July 15.	" six months' interest on $3,800 U. S. 7 3-10 bonds,	138 70
" 15.	" cash of H. H. Learnard, Town Treasurer, in part for Town appropriation for 1867,	500 00
Aug. 13.	" cash of Librarian for fines, 3 mos. ending Aug. 1,	20 27
Nov. 22.	" cash of Librarian for fines, 3 mos. ending Nov. 1,	19 27
" 30.	" cash difference of int. on conversion of bonds,	5 17
1868.		
Feb. 4.	" cash of H. H. Learnard, Town Treasurer, in part for Town appropriation for 1867,	500 00
" 10.	" cash of Librarian for fines, 3 mos. ending Feb. 1,	12 89
		$5,079 81

Cr.

1868.		
May 15.	By cash paid Cambridge Chronicle bill,	$ 7 00
" 15.	" W. F. Warren, bill of sundries,	11 87
" 17.	" Hooper, Lewis & Co., bill of paper,	10 20
July 25.	" Nichols & Noyes, bill of books,	93 35
" 30.	" Check Stamps,	50
Aug. 6.	" W. S. Bartlett, bill of books,	16 37
" 13.	" Nichols & Noyes, bill of books,	83 32
Oct. 10.	" W. F. Warren, bill of sundries,	11 31
" 17.	" Rev. F. A. Whitney, bill of books,	13 60
" 17.	" Nichols & Noyes, bill of books,	45 47
" 17.	" Hooper, Lewis & Co., bill of books,	5 50
Nov. 22.	" J. P. C. Winship, bill of books,	3 50
	" W. F. Warren, bill of sundries,	11 70
1868.		
Jan. 23.	" J. A. Sinclair, bill of sundries,	3 75
Feb. 3.	" Covert & Co., bill of books,	3 00
" 4.	" Hooper, Lewis & Co., bill of paper, &c.	2 00
" 6.	" W. S. Bartlott, bill of books,	17 42
" 6.	" Nichols & Noyes, bill of books,	155 64
" 10.	" W. F. Warren, bill of sundries,	6 00
	Balance on hand,	4,578 31
		$5,079 81

Respectfully submitted by

L. BALDWIN, *Treasurer.*

FIFTH ANNUAL REPORT

OF THE

TRUSTEES

OF THE

HOLTON LIBRARY,

BRIGHTON,

FEBRUARY 1st, 1869.

BOSTON:
ROCKWELL & ROLLINS PRINTERS,
122 WASHINGTON STREET.
1869.

FIFTH ANNUAL REPORT

OF THE

TRUSTEES

OF THE

HOLTON LIBRARY,

BRIGHTON,

FEBRUARY 1st, 1869.

BOSTON:
ROCKWELL & ROLLINS PRINTERS,
122 WASHINGTON STREET.
1869.

TOWN OF BRIGHTON.

HOLTON LIBRARY, *Feb.* 1, 1869.

TO THE AUDITORS:

Gentlemen: — I have the honor to transmit to you, herewith, the Fifth Annual Report of the Trustees of the Holton Library, prepared in obedience to the Ordinance adopted by the town, April 8, 1864.

Yours respectfully,

B. S. FISKE,
Secretary of the Board of Trustees.

TRUSTEES

Of the Library from its Commencement.

BALDWIN, LIFE	1864
BENYON, ABNER INGALLS	1866–68
BICKFORD, WEARE DOW	1864
BRECK, CHARLES HENRY BASS	1867
CUSHMAN, JOHN PAINE	1864–66
FISKE, BELA STODDARD	1865
FULLER, GRANVILLE	1864
HUTCHINSON, CHARLES CARROLL	1864–65
JACKSON, NATHANIEL	1864
MATCHETT, THEODORE	1864–67
MATCHETT, WILLIAM FREDERICK	1867
POND, JOSEPH ADAMS	1864–67
RICE, EDMUND	1865
RUGGLES, JOHN	1864–65
WARREN, WEBSTER FRANKLIN	1869
WARREN, WILLIAM WIRT	1864
WHITNEY, FREDERICK AUGUSTUS	1864
WINSHIP, JOHN PERKINS CUSHING	1864

OFFICERS

Of the Library from its Commencement.

PRESIDENTS.

JOHN RUGGLES,	April 18, 1864 — October 9, 1865.
FREDERIC AUGUSTUS WHITNEY,	November 13, 1865 —

SECRETARIES.

JOHN PERKINS CUSHING WINSHIP,	April 18, 1864 — March 13, 1865.
BELA STODDARD FISKE,	March 13, 1865.

TREASURER.

LIFE BALDWIN,	May 23, 1864 —

LIBRARIANS.

JOHN PERKINS CUSHING WINSHIP,	June 13, 1864 — July 9, 1866.
WEBSTER FRANKLIN WARREN,	July 9, 1866 —

FIFTH ANNUAL REPORT

OF THE

TRUSTEES OF THE HOLTON LIBRARY.

In obedience to the Ordinance respecting the Holton Library, adopted by the Town of Brighton, April 8, 1864, the Trustees have the honor to submit their Fifth Annual

REPORT.

The institution has received through another year the continued sympathy and favor of our citizens. On each appointed day and evening of delivery the cards of subscribers, comprising the young, the middle-aged, and the old, have been numerously presented. And it appears accordingly that the books, as welcome guests, have, in these twelve months, gone in and out among the homes of our people, in number, if we duplicate the books by their visits, between seventeen and eighteen thousand volumes.

I. OBSERVANCE OF THE RULES AND REGULATIONS.

We have felt it a privilege to administer a trust so conducive, it is believed, to the enjoyment and improvement of the community. Those using the Library during the past year have very generally and harmoniously acquiesced in the standing Rules and Regulations which were at first borrowed, as far as applicable, from those of the Boston Public Library

and of a few other public libraries which preceded our
own. The small number of volumes lost, the few instances
of abuse or undue detention of books, which will be presented
in the Librarian's Report, we may, for the present at least,
offset with the advantages of a circulation so free. Article
10, Chapter II., of the printed Rules and Regulations, forbidding conversation in the Reading Room, is, perhaps, more
frequently infringed than others, if not always in outspoken
words, yet in very audible whisperings, especially in the
evening. If to any young persons the pleasantly warmed
and lighted hall offers attractions beyond those of the reviews and magazines and volumes of reference, we must remind such that infringement of the rules, of right deprives
them of the privileges of the Library. The Librarian in his
report has brought to the notice of the Board some instances
of disturbance by conversation. We shall expect the attend-
ants to report the names of any of whom complaint is thus
made. It seems unnecessary to add that every person using
the Library has first promised to obey the Rules and Regulations, by signing them; without which act, no card can be
given. In case of wilful disobedience, the Board has no
choice, as the servants of the town in executing the town's
trust, but to enforce the Regulations and withdraw the card.
It is stated that in the Boston Library "of the cards granted
during the year, thirty-three were reclaimed for good rea-
sons."

II. BOARD OF TRUSTEES.

Of the Board of Trustees, as at first constituted, twelve in
all, the official term of four, or one-third, expires each year.
At the annual town meeting in March, 1868, Messrs. Warren (William Wirt), Breck, Fuller, and Winship, who retired, were re-elected for a period of three years. One
vacancy on the Board has been occasioned by the removal
from town, in October last, of Mr. Benyon. Mr. Webster

Franklin Warren was subsequently chosen in his place. The term of office of Messrs. Whitney, Bickford, Warren (Webster Franklin) and Jackson will expire in March, 1869, when the town will again elect.

III. OFFICERS, BOOKS, DONATIONS.

At the meeting of the Trustees, the first after the Annual Town Meeting in March, 1868, officers were chosen as required by the By-Laws. The President, Secretary, Treasurer, and Librarian of the previous year were re-elected. Frederic Augustus, son of Horace William Pierce, and Hiram Norton, son of Hiram Cushman, still pursuing their studies in the High School, have again been employed as assistants to the Librarian. The Librarian's Report accompanies this, and, with other statistical information, enumerates as the number of volumes belonging to the Library on the first of February, 1869, five thousand and eight. Of pamphlets unbound, there are one thousand one hundred and eighty-five. This number includes periodicals, reviews, and magazines of 1868, which will immediately be bound and go upon the shelves as additional volumes. Sixty-six volumes and one hundred and twenty pamphlets were presented to the Library the past year. The names of all the donors are given in tabular form by the Librarian, and certified letters of thankful acknowledgment on behalf of the Trustees have been returned.

To one of their own number, Mr. William F. Matchett, his associates on the Board would tender their especial thanks for a costly volume, in royal octavo, just from the press, on "Mines and Miners." It is a work of great authority, translated from the French of Louis Simonin, by H. W. Bristow, F.R.S., of the Geological Survey, Honorary Fellow of King's College, London. The underground life of multitudes of English and European operatives is here shown with entire faithfulness to the figures, and persons, and animals, and implements employed in the various processes of mining.

Plate 154, — "Miners at Prayer, at la Vieille, Montagne, before descending the Shaft," in which fifteen persons, male and female, are shown in their mining costume — impresses the beholder. Illustrated with one hundred and sixty engravings, many of them the size of the page, with twenty maps, geologically colored, and with plates of metals and minerals in chromolithograph, this volume enriches the Library as a valuable book of reference. Of course, works of this expense, presented usually on condition of being kept at the Library, cannot go into general circulation, but must be consulted with care, and read by those asking for them on the tables of the hall.

Besides our own citizens, others have made contributions. Our Senator in Congress, Hon. Charles Sumner, and our Representative, Hon. George Sewall Boutwell, have continued to increase our collections of Congressional and other Public Documents. The publications of the Boston, Manchester, and Worcester Public Libraries, and of others, have been kindly furnished by their officers. Mrs. John S. Tyler, of Boston, has again made a donation to the Library of the town, which, though not her birthplace, as was stated in the last Report, was the birthplace of her father, the late Mr. Abiel Winship, her own residence for a time, and the home of branches of her family for many years. As expressions of a generous sympathy and co-operation in the institution more than as a matter of pecuniary necessity, these contributions, to which attention has been more fully called in former reports, are most gratefully acknowledged and solicited from our citizens.

IV. FINANCES.

The Fifth Annual Report of the Treasurer, Mr. Baldwin, is likewise appended. The receipts for the year are detailed, including the appropriation made by the town at the last annual meeting. The sums expended for books, paper, and sundries for the Library are likewise given. The amount rendered for the services of the Librarian and assistants, being a town charge, appear in the annual report of the Town Treasurer, as do also the charges for coal and gas, and general repairs on the building.

V. ALCOVES BUILT — BUILDING WANTED.

We have been obliged to provide additional shelf-room, during the year. This was done by erecting six alcoves on the east side of the inner hall, similar to those which were erected, in 1865, on the north side. Provision is thus made for many more volumes, and the additional alcoves rather improve the appearance of the hall. Still, neat and commodious as the two halls are at present, as described more particularly in the Trustees' second Report, it must not be forgotten, that, in extent but about seventy feet, they will soon be quite insufficient for the accommodation of the Library. The edifice used for a Public Library should be devoted to that purpose alone, and this alike on the ground of freedom from noise and other interruptions, and from exposure to fire. The large hall for town purposes embraces the entire story above our halls. The basement story of the edifice is appropriated to the police department. And still in another portion of the building, above the basement, are rooms for the town officers. We need exceedingly a fire-proof edifice standing apart, where these treasures, becoming each year more valuable, may be safely kept.

VI. NEW EDIFICE AT BROOKLINE.

We cannot but feel this need the more, as on either side of us, at Brookline and at Newton, such noble edifices are already in process of completion for the Public Libraries of those towns. That at Brookline is on Washington Street, near the Town Hall, standing back about one hundred feet from the street, to be approached, as described on the plan of the architect, Mr. Louis Weissbein, by two wide walks which will encircle an ornamental grass-plot with a fountain in the centre. Broad granite steps will lead to a portico in sandstone, communicating with a vestibule some fourteen feet by six. From the vestibule, a large door leads to the waiting-room, which is thirty-four feet by fifteen. Opposite the entrance will be the Librarian's office, seventeen feet by fourteen. Connected with the waiting-room on the right will be the reading-room, thirty-three feet by twenty. On the left of the office will be the Librarian's room, twenty feet by twelve. The library-room, which forms a wing to the main edifice, is on the rear of the office, forty-five feet by thirty-two, and eighteen feet in height. It will have galleries, approached by two spiral staircases, with alcoves above and below. The upper, or Mansard story, beneath the French roof, will be ten feet in height, comprising a hall, a room for the Trustees, and one for the Superintendent, and a storage room. In the basement, which will be nine feet high, will be a work-room, packing-room, furnace-room, etc.

The edifice is of brick, with sandstone trimmings over a granite basement; to cost about thirty-five thousand dollars and to be occupied during the coming summer.

VII. NEW EDIFICE AT NEWTON.

The fine edifice at Newton, on Centre Street, likewise in process of erection, is the fruit of individual subscriptions. We gladly record here the munificent generosity of the Hon. J. Wiley Edmunds, of that place, who, in January, 1868, offered to contribute the sum of fifteen thousand dollars towards the establishment of a free Public Library, upon condition that a like sum should be raised by the first of March ensuing. This condition was more than fulfilled in the collection of nearly twenty-two thousand dollars; when Mr. Edmunds placed fifteen thousand, as promised, at the disposal of the Trustees of the Newton Library Association. He also furnished, through Mr. A. R. Esty, architect, plans for a building. Ground was broken on the tenth of June last and, in the presence of a great assembly, the cornerstone of what will be a commodious and elegant structure was laid on the twelfth of August. The admirable address by the Rev. Edward James Young, delivered on the occasion, and the other appropriate services which were shared by the Rev. Messrs. Tucker, Wellman, and Rogers, clergymen, likewise of Newton, and by Mr. George H. Jones of the Trustees, and not least the beautiful hymn written for the day by the Rev. Mr. Tarbox, — all testify to the deep interest felt by the town in this most commendable work. As described in the architect's plan, the building is of stone from quarries in Newton, — the cornices, window-finish, etc., in stone from Hallowell, Maine. It is of two stories, — the first being sixty by forty feet for a reading and for a conversation room, and for commodious closets. The upper story is to be devoted to the Library and Trustees' room. The library-room will be twenty-four feet in height, with galleries. The edifice, in the Venetian Gothic style of architecture, cannot fail to be an ornament, as in its object it will be an honor, the worthiest to the town.

VIII. SUBSCRIPTIONS FOR LIBRARY AT WATERTOWN, AND DONATION TO THE PUBLIC LIBRARY AT LYNN.

Mention was made, in the last Report, of a movement in Watertown for the establishment of a free Public Library when the sum of six thousand dollars should be obtained by subscription, — the same sum which the generous founder of our Library, Mr. Holton, at first bequeathed. That amount having been obtained, the Library is about to be opened in apartments in the Town Hall. Among the contributors to the above-named fund, we have seen published the names of Mr. Alvin Adams in the sum of one thousand dollars, of Mr. J. A. Locke of six hundred dollars, and of Mr. H. H. Hunnewell, and of the heirs of the late Abijah White, of five hundred dollars each. And, even while writing this, we learn, from the daily prints, of similar generosity in one of our young cities, — namely, that the late Sidney B. Pratt has left a bequest of ten thousand dollars for the benefit of the free Public Library at Lynn.

IX. A MUNIFICENT BEQUEST.

It is well that the good deeds of the benefactors of their race should be widely known and remembered alike for encouragement and emulation; and we must be permitted to mention here one most laudable example more, in connection with libraries for the people. While our illustrious countryman, Mr. George Peabody, has of late awakened the admiration of the world in his unexampled bequests, alike for philanthropic and for educational purposes, both at home and abroad, in a far humbler way to be sure, but in the same great spirit, has another noble man marked the past year with a princely donation for a Public Library in his native town. We refer to Mr. Augustine Heard, who died on the fourteenth of September last, at his residence in Ipswich in this State, at the ripe age of fourscore years and three, beloved, as few have been, for his singularly unselfish heart. Beginning life, his biographer tells us, as an apprentice in a mercantile house, and then going as supercargo to Calcutta, he became one of Boston's ablest ship-masters. He was for many years connected with the house of Russell & Co.; but at length established a house of his own, with branches at all the principal trading ports of China. Though with his advancing years he retired himself from the house, it is still in the hands of his nephews, and in his name, one of the ablest and most successful commercial establishments in the China trade. His days had been devoted to good deeds; and all charitable and benevolent objects found in him a ready patron. And, as the crowning glory of his long and useful life, let it be told here, that a large library and building, fitted up at a cost of not less than fifty thousand dollars, was ready for dedication on the week after his death, which he had prepared as a free gift to the people of Ipswich, the place of his birth.

Commending these various instances of marked generosity in a most deserving cause to the favorable regards of the many among us possessed of ample means, we pass to the consideration of

X. THE CARE AND PRESERVATION OF THE BOOKS.

In no subject connected with the Library ought the citizens to feel a livelier interest than in this. These books are theirs. These treasures, every day accumulating, entrusted, indeed, to the oversight and management of their twelve agents, are, nevertheless, their own property, instruments for their highest enjoyment and improvement. It is right that they hold their trustees, who consent so to serve, strictly responsible for the care and preservation of these collections. Of course, the very existence and possession of the institution is involved in its care. To be sure, some books are lost and some are unduly injured. Still, we are glad to report the condition of the Library so favorable in this respect as we may. But no solicitation of ours can be untimely that all receiving the books would more and more zealously co-operate for their careful use and for their safe and punctual return.

XI. PRACTICE AT THE BOSTON PUBLIC LIBRARY.

At the Boston Public Library much attention has been bestowed on this subject. The damage there by loss and injury, though by no means excessive, has resulted in the adoption of more stringent regulations than at first, and every one taking a card, as borrower, must now give the names of two responsible persons as vouchers for his integrity.

Those, also, consulting the periodicals, reviews, magazines, and books of reference on the tables, must apply to an attendant for what they wish, and are held responsible for its return before leaving the hall.

Whatever might be thought of such regulations in smaller communities, they are not without reasonable justification in a great city, like Boston, as shown in the following extracts from the Superintendent's last Report: —

"It was apparent that in a public institution we must require this of *everybody*, and it was hoped no umbrage would be taken at so reasonable a course, which was the only way in which the library could escape the imputation of granting class-privileges. It is not known that the asking of these two names has kept away a single person who *could not* give them; but some who *would not* have foregone its privileges rather than do this penance for the public good. It must be remembered that the founders of the library contemplated much more stringent measures than these. The preliminary Report of 1852 recommended pecuniary guaranties from persons not personally or reputably known; and it was this Report that induced Mr. Bates to do what he did." [Give fifty thousand dollars to the Library.] . . . "It is a fact that all libraries of any considerable size find it necessary to go farther than we now go in the matter of guaranties. Libraries of colleges are secured by the bonds given by their students. Corporated libraries have the stock and assessments of their shareholders to depend upon. Libraries of Congress and States have prior claims upon the pay of legislators. Ought not public libraries, throwing open their collections to all, to have some protection? There are nearly sixty free public libraries in the towns and lesser cities of Massachusetts; and the practice is usual with them (where the chances of knowing personally the applicants are much greater than in a city like Boston) to demand vouchers, particularly for minors. The Public Library of Cincinnati demands a deposit of three dollars from its citizens who wish to use its books."

Such regulations as adopted at the City Library are highly salutary. Who will not rejoice in every new check which is thus thrown in the way of dishonesty and recklessness? And though, as we learn, some few in Boston complain, no right-minded person, it would seem, could object to regulations so wholesome, especially when told, as in the last communication from the annual examining committee of the Boston Library to the trustees, that since their adoption,

" only one-seventh part of the number of books that was formerly lost, is lost now."

The able Report of Mr. Justin Winsor, the Superintendent of the Boston Library has been lately communicated to the public by the trustees. That institution sustained a serious loss in the sudden death of its late accomplished superintendent, Mr. Charles C. Jewett, on the 9th of January, 1868. Professor William Everett Jillson, the general assistant, was appointed in his place. Ill health prevented his acceptance; and he, too, was removed by death on the 27th of November last. The departure, almost simultaneously, of two men so gifted and so fitted for the stations which they adorned, claims the respectful sympathy of every lover of good learning and general knowledge. Mr. Winsor, selected from the Board of Trustees to fill the office thus vacated, has presented most thoroughly in this his first Report, the condition of the Library. By the aid of statistical tables of comparison with other public libraries, large and small, in this country and abroad, and with most loving zeal and care, he has performed his work to the utter discomfiture of all superficialists in similar departments of service. We shall not hesitate to transfer to these pages one or two of his statistical tables, in which our own Library is counted, for the information of our citizens. The complete series of the Boston Public Library Reports may be found on our shelves.

On this subject of which we are treating, — the care and preservation of books, — Mr. Winsor presents an interesting table that comprises statistics from the Library of Brighton, and of ten other towns and cities, prefacing it with the following judicious remarks on the wisdom of strict regulations for the prevention of injury and loss.

"We learn from the Franklin Society, in Paris, that those libraries which it has nurtured throughout France, have all failed in which there was laxity in this respect. The officers of the law can call upon citizens to help preserve the peace; and can we not expect from our frequenters, — at even a little inconvenience to themselves, — that they will help us by conforming to wholesome rules, in the work of preservation and discipline which we have to do? Where the individual suffers, the community gains. We deal here with a large proportion of the youth of the city. If they find they can abuse, with impunity, the public treasures here kept, they may learn to believe that public possessions of other kinds are accumulated for individual cupidity. It is a question more often put to me than any other by strangers, what protection do you have in lending a book? When it is remembered that the institution opens its doors very wide to all the inhabitants of a large city, all that are not confused in their notions of liberty and license must see that this question of strangers is a natural one, and that there may be grave misgivings with such, at the risk of such freedom as we accord. But the fact that our experience is no worse than it is, must not mislead us into ignoring what it actually is. Our early reports show that it was felt our immunity from abuse was surprising; but the abuse crept in, as it always will with familiarity and trial of impunity. . . The danger of increasing wontedness to the library is well illustrated in the flourishing institution at Charlestown. Last year their loss was double what it was three years before, although their circulation had diminished one-quarter.

"The loss in libraries depends largely upon the efficiency of such disciplinary measures with the takers. The following list is cited as showing a comparative statement of losses in several libraries of different grades, sizes, or degrees of exact management. The first column of figures shows the loss their circulation should have borne to be relative to ours. The second column is what they actually did lose.

	Vols.	Vols.
" Beverly Public Library,	2 to 3	10 to 15
Holton (Brighton) Library,	10 to 12	10 to 12
Stoneham Public Library,	3 to 4	25
Charlestown Public Library,	12 to 13	14
Lynn Public Library,	10 to 11	62
Northampton Public Library,	2 to 3	12
New Bedford Public Library,	8	35
Syracuse (N. Y.) Public Library,	7	13
New York Mercantile Library,	51	300
San Francisco Mercantile Library,	15	125
Providence Athenæum,	4 to 5	12 to 20 "

It appears from the above table of Mr. Winsor, that our *ratio* of damage by loss and injury, as returned in our Librarian's Report (1868), was just the same as that of the Boston Library, while the ratio of damage in each of the other libraries counted in the table, was greater; in some, as in Lynn, New York, and San Francisco, very much greater.

XII. AVERAGE NO. OF VOLUMES TAKEN BY EACH PERSON.

Our citizens may be interested to know how far our cardholders actually use the Library as compared with the borrowers in other towns; and Mr. Winsor's tables must again help us in this comparison. He says that the persons in Boston, who used the lower hall, which contains over twenty-six thousand volumes, and is the only portion of the Library open for public borrowers, took out, on an average, thirteen volumes in the year. Our Librarian returned in February, 1868, for the year then closed, an average number of twenty-one (20 9-10) books to each borrower. During the past year, the average, as shown in our statistics, has not been quite as large as in the preceding year, — some cardholders having taken very few, and some, probably, having removed from town. In this table, Mr. Winsor has shown the average number of volumes to each borrower in several towns and cities, compiled, it is presumed, from their annual returns, or Reports.

PUBLIC LIBRARIES IN MASSACHUSETTS.

Lynn,	44	Fall River,	13
Dana (Cambridge),	43	Leominster,	13
South Reading,	34	Northampton,	13
Weston,	30	Waltham,	12
Wayland,	27	Winchester,	12
Holton (Brighton),	20	Brookline,	10
Fitchburg,	19	Concord,	10
New Bedford,	17	Newburyport,	9
Phillipston,	14	Beverly,	8
Taunton,	14	Westford,	6
Stoneham,	13		

Considerable difference is shown in these averages. The Superintendent, who prepared the table, suggests that it may be in part explained in the fact that in some of the smaller places only the heads of families sign and receive cards. But, with us, boys and girls of a prescribed age, as well as heads of families, receive cards as in Boston; and our number, 20, in the above table, expresses the average delivery to each man, woman, and young person holding a card.

XIII. DEFACEMENT OF BOOK—COVERS.

With such steady circulation of the books, as shown above, the covers, unless constantly replenished, must be often considerably worn. We are asked, can you not more frequently renew them? Those asking are hardly aware of the amount of labor already rendered in this department. By providing, as we shall, more duplicates of the most popular books, this evil will be somewhat remedied. We have found great satisfaction in our practice, lately adopted, of printing on the paper coverings of the books, as fast as they require recovering, a few of the established regulations which most affect borrowers. Although complete copies of the Rules and Regulations are delivered to every family, they may not always be at hand. The complaint of soiled covers is, probably, incident to every public library. We are told, in the last Boston Report, of the "untidy condition" into which popular books there fall, "as giving some a distaste for frequenting the hall." In this hall for popular delivery, are about twenty-six thousand volumes, of which, perhaps, some do not go out, or but rarely, in a year. Yet, of this collection, the Superintendent writes thus, in justification: —

"When our records show that thirty-five thousand new paper covers were put upon these books during the past year, it would indicate that considerable assiduity is experienced to keep the outside of the books presentable. A large number have had their bindings repaired or renewed, and two hundred and fifty-seven volumes have been condemned."

The best remedy, after all, for this universal complaint must be found — who sees not? — in the increased care of borrowers. We may cover and renew, but without this home-care, the volume in its tidiest and freshest dress, may be soiled in a day.

XIV. BOOKS ADDED LAST YEAR.

Since the printing of the catalogue in 1866, supplements only have been furnished for use at the hall. The issue of extra sheets for the catalogues, to which reference was made last year, is delayed a little for further entries. The Trustees desire to add continually such books as will most profit and most worthily entertain. They must again call attention to the record-book at the Librarian's desk, in which any card-holder desiring a book not already belonging, may enter its title with his or her name, and it will be procured. A good proportion of the leading standard works in the popular literature of England and America are already on the shelves, and we seek now to bring in the best as they come fresh from the press, in the various departments of bibliography, wishing that none which the people are reading may escape. All works possessed in sets and in series we aim to keep complete as each year passes. The reviews, magazines, and other periodicals which, while in parts, are for reference and reading in the hall, only, — at the close of the year are bound, and become books of delivery. Of course, it were not desirable in any of our town libraries to purchase many works in any other than the English tongue. But the supplements will show that in history and politics, American and foreign; in biography and travels; in fiction, poetry, and rhetoric; in theology; in moral, intellectual, and physical science; in military and naval science; in geography and natural history; in oratory (would not the fourth and last grand volume of Mr. Everett's works, lately entered from the press, here make a class in itself, if we had entered no other?) ; in the useful and in the fine arts, — the past year has made some rich accessions to the Library, whose organization is yet so recent.

XV. WORKS OF FICTION HERE AND ELSEWHERE.

People everywhere, the young and the old, still love to read fiction. From the establishment of this institution, the works of many of the best writers in this department have been on the shelves, and accordingly their publications of the past year have been added. In this Library the proportion of works of fiction to other books is not quite as large as in some other public libraries, as shown in the returns which have been made to Mr. Winsor, at Boston. Our frequent reference to his tables and his authority must be set down simply to the account that he has done his work so well. Indeed, his results, obtained by extensive comparison and correspondence, ought to be widely disseminated by every one interested in the subject of public libraries. He shows us that the demand for and the prevalence of works of fiction, in the public libraries of this country and abroad, is far greater than most persons suppose. At the hall of general delivery, in the Boston Library, he says : —

"Fiction in English constitutes something over thirty per cent. of the whole collection, and this, apparently by no predetermination, coincides with what, on an average, seems to be judged best for the service of public libraries. From the kind responses to my inquiries which have been made so generally by the librarians of the numerous public and other libraries in this State and elsewhere, here and in Europe, I find that in Massachusetts it is just about the average percentage given by these libraries to fiction in their annual purchases, though the practices of individual libraries range from five per cent. to sixty-six per cent., and for our library, the past year, fiction has constituted more than fifty per cent. of its additions. Again, comparing these same libraries in our lesser cities and towns, it will appear that these issues of fiction range from twenty-five per cent. to eighty-three per cent., fixing an average at about fifty-five per cent. Furthermore the extent of their use of fiction is almost always in direct accordance with the extent of their purchases in this department. The library (Lynn) which buys most largely (sixty per cent.) of fiction has the largest proportion of such use (eighty-three per cent). . . . . .

"At the New York Mercantile Library, where they supply duplicates on a liberal scale not elsewhere attempted, they follow this rule in buying: —

"'Of novels, if six fruitless calls are made daily for an old title, three or four additional copies are added. If from twenty-five to fifty such calls for a new novel are made daily, ten to fifteen new copies are added. Of books not novels, a new copy is added for every two calls daily which cannot be met.'

"This same preponderance prevails in England. At the public library at Oxford, their purchases are thirty-three per cent.; at Salford, fiction forming fifty per cent. of its lending libraries, makes ninety per cent. of its issues; at Liverpool, seventy-one per cent.; while at Sheffield, it is only forty-seven per cent. .

"In France the proportion of fiction is fixed by the Franklin Society — an institution that ought to be copied among us — at much the same as with us. This society, in founding and encouraging libraries throughout France, establishes for their guidance the principle that of every twenty volumes, seven should be fiction, five travels, four history, and four in science.

"With us, then, for the past year [Boston Library] it appears that each volume of fiction has found thirteen readers, while all other books in this hall got less than two."

And in view of this so universal taste, the Superintendent proceeds with an eloquent plea in behalf of fiction as, when judiciously employed, a great instrument in the education of the race, and a "craving not of low minds alone." The authorities which he cites, and the force of his reasoning, the indiscriminate denouncers of all works of fiction will not easily gainsay.

But then it is to be *judiciously* employed. Let not this qualifying term be overlooked. The most constant readers of fiction exercise little or no judgment in the matter. They often lose all relish for works of real and lasting worth. The condiment is not employed to flavor, but substituted for the nutritious food. Let just proportions be observed here, lest the good powers of the mind be enervated and the good hours of life squandered. A quaint physiologist said to his pupils in reference to different articles of food, "Consider always how they will mix." It is well that Scott, Dickens, Bulwer, Curtis, Mitchell, Winthrop, Arthur, Austen, Brontë and Evans, Cooper and Edgeworth, Hawthorne and Holmes, Marryat and Reid and Reade, Thackeray and Thoreau, Muhlbach and Muloch, Southworth and Warner and Wood, and their followers, legion, all mix, say with Hume and Hallam and Macaulay, with Sparks, Bancroft, Prescott and Motley, with poets and biographers, with philosophers, moralists, essayists, with the grand leaders in all departments of thought, even though the latter sometimes task the faculties.

Occasionally, it may be, a taste for the lighter forms of literature leads one up to the weightier authors, when, without this beginning, one had read nothing. If possible, let us in this way look for good out of seeming evil. On the other hand, not quite judicious seems to us the advice of Lord Sheffield, Duke of Buckinghamshire, in his essay on Poetry, who, self-taught for the most part, and sharing in the din of war, yet neglecting never the pursuits of letters, became, some two hundred years ago, one of England's ripe scholars, living into the Augustan age of English literature under Queen Anne. He would dictate, rather, that the mind, once tasting the master-writers of song or prose, would never desire inferior authors. Thus he charges:—

> "Read Homer once, and you can read no more,
> For all books else appear so mean, so poor;
> Verse will seem prose, but still persist to read,
> And Homer will be all the books you need."

But, notwithstanding the scholar-duke and tolerably good poet, we counsel rather the mixing process. Accordingly, with the additions made the past year in works of fiction, have gone also, and far more numerously, upon the shelves such other books as considerations of permanent value and general utility and popular demand required.

XVI. CHARACTER OF BOOKS ADDED OTHER THAN FICTION.

Some of these, from their value, or from their numerous plates, or from conditions of bequest, must be necessarily books of reference. Such is the Pictorial History of the Great Rebellion, just added, in two folio volumes, enriched with one ~~hundred~~ *thousand* illustrations, many of them the size of the book, some sixteen inches by twelve. The remaining books are free to all borrowers. And the issues from the American and English press alone, in twelve months only, from which we may select, how numerous! All pathos has long since gone out from those early words of King Solomon in the book of Ecclesiastes, in which our childish compassion was wont to be awakened for that "son" of his, whose "weariness of the flesh" was induced, we supposed, by the "much study" of the "many books," of the "making of" which his wise father "admonished" him there was "no end." Why, how that son's flesh would have ached to have read a tithe of the books of to-day!

Another volume of the Life and Works of Jefferson, to be comprised in nine royal octavo volumes, has been added to the Library, and likewise the third volume of the Life and Times of Madison, in similar style; fit companions both, for the works already there of Washington and John Adams, the earlier, and of others, the later presidents of our nation. John Milton and his Times; Hazlitt's Table Talk of Luther, and the Table Talk of Napoleon; Greeley's Recollection of a Busy Life; the third and last volume of Kirk's History of Charles the Bold; White's Life and Writings of Swedenborg; and Light on the Last Things, a Swedenborgian treatise, by William B. Hayden — are on the supplements. On opening the latter volume, at a chapter headed "The visible heavens not to be destroyed — the stars too large to fall to the earth," it occurred to us to ask why, in the event of the destruction of the universe, if the law of gravity be universal, the earth might not as well fall to the stars, as the stars to the earth? The works of Richard Cobden, in two volumes; the miscellaneous prose works of Bulwer, statesman, essayist, poet and novelist, likewise, in two; Abbott's History of Napoleon III., and the Life of John Sullivan, by Amory — the year has given us. That brave book, What Answer? by Anna E. Dickinson, of which, among other noted and most favorable critics, Mrs. Stowe writes, "What gives this story its awful power is its truth," and of which the publishers certify that twenty thousand copies went out in twenty days, is added. So, too, have we added the deeply interesting Life — edited by Mrs. Sarah H. Bradford — of that deliverer of her oppressed people, Harriet Tubman. Stranger indeed than fiction seems this unvarnished tale of truth. This heroine, for her loyal and daring services during the war as scout, guide, and nurse, has well won the title of a second Joan of Arc.

Maxwell's Life of the Duke of Wellington, an English edition, in two volumes, illustrated; Life in the Argentine Republic; Perry's Carthage and Tunis Past and Present; St. Augustine, Florida; Reminiscences of European Travel, by Rev. Dr. Peabody of the University, most instructive and entertaining; and the second volume of the Old World in it's New Face, by Rev. Henry Whitney Bellows, D. D., with the first volume of which the public has been already so favorably impressed, — have been supplied. To Rev. Robert Collier's Nature and Life, already so favorably received, we have added A Man in Earnest, by the same gifted author. For those who love to feast the eye while instructing the mind, The Gallery of Nature, pictorial and descriptive, a large London edition, offers attractions. The Turkish Empire; Nevius' Life in China; Dyer's finely illustrated work on Pompeii, and the second volume of Kinglake's Invasion of the Crimea, are among the contributions of the year.

Resources of the Pacific Slope, a statistical and descriptive summary of the mines and minerals, climate, topography, agriculture, commerce, manufactures, and productions of the States and Territories west of the Rocky Mountains; likewise The Natural Wealth of California; and Five Years within the Golden Gates,—have been added to the many works already possessed on that important region. President Hopkins' late Lowell Lectures, in book form, entitled, The Law of Love and Love as Law, open a field of moral science most comprehensive. Rev. Dr. Bushnell's work, on the Moral Uses of Dark Things, is food most nutritious, with all the seasoning that can be asked, and will not fail to shed blessed light in many darkened minds. Read, all ye from whose outward intercourse beloved ones have passed behind the veil, his chapter on Non-Intercourse Between Worlds, and it will not be the only chapter you will read. And the Gates Ajar, by Miss Phelps,—how from perusal of these pages is heaven brought very near, and how tender an interest in the spiritual world is unconsciously awakened by its beautiful religious spirit!

The Letters of Madame De Sevigné and those of Lady Mary Wortley Montagu, selected and arranged by Mrs. Sarah J. Hale, and The Story of my Childhood, by Madame J. Michelet, form three most attractive volumes. Cuvier's Animal Kingdom, the four large works from the French of Louis Figuier, all copiously illustrated, namely, The Insect World, The World before the Deluge, The Vegetable World, and the Ocean World; and Michelet's elegantly illustrated treatise, called The Bird,—are among the contributions of the past year to Natural History. A Summer in Iceland, by one of the Professors in the University of Upisal, Sweden, is an illustrated octavo volume. It is said there is no other book in the English tongue, on Iceland, a country concerning which we all wish to learn, so instructive and entertaining as this. Travels and Adventures in South and Central America, by Don Ramon Paez, takes the reader into new scenes where he may learn and enjoy much. Curiosities of the Pulpit, edited by Thomas Jackson, of London, is defined as a most entertaining "collection of the grandeur and quaintness, the humor and pathos of the pulpit, from the days of St. Augustine and St. Basil to those of Chalmers and Beecher." A book about Dominies, by Hope, to all schoolteachers especially attractive, with his book about Boys; A Half Century with Juvenile Delinquents, by Rev. B. K. Pierce, D.D.; and Glimpses of Prison Life, by Gideon Haynes, Warden of the Massachusetts State Prison; Moore's Rebellion Record, volumes nine, ten, and eleven, in continuation of the previous volumes on hand; the second elegant volume of Professor Draper's History of the Civil War, to be completed in a third; Abbott's Life of Napoleon III.; Lossing's richly illustrated History of the United States, with some five-hundred engravings, — are all instructive and readable. In two rich-looking octavo volumes come the Speeches of John Bright, bearing the stamp of the printers to the University of Oxford. In Parliament both parties count him the first orator in the House of Commons. Our late rebellion told the loyal people of the United States where he stood, — their sincere and earnest friend. Seven of these speeches are on America. As models in rhetoric and oratory they should be read with those of our own Everett, by every young man ambitions to serve his country.

Watchwords for the Warfare of Life, by the gifted authoress of the Schonberg-Cotta Family, Mrs. Charles; and Patience Strong's Outings, by Mrs. Whitney, — the former publications of both being already in the Library, — have been added, and are attracting the attention of thoughtful readers more and more. Miss Alcott's Little Women; Horatio Alger's Fame and Fortune; William Everett's Changing Base; If, Yes, and Perhaps, by Rev. Edward E. Hale; Cameos from English History; Wild Life under the Equator, by Chailln; and Miss Bremer's Life in the Old World, — are all additions to former works from these authors. For those regardful of health, we have put in from the contributions of the past year, Professor Dalton's Treatise on Physiology and Hygiene; Parton's Smoking and Drinking; Plain Thoughts on the Art of Living, by Gladden; Anthracite Coal and Health, by Dr. George Derby, which all house-keepers who keep inner doors closed, will do well to consult; The Philosophy of Eating, and How Not to be Sick, by a physician, Dr. Bellows. Tablets, by Mr. Alcott, will be especially commended by pupils of the Emersonian School. Gould's Treatise on the Genius of the elder Booth, illustrated by a fine portrait from the author's marble bust of his subject, nearly a score of years since deceased, must not suffer in the reading, in the consideration of the sad career and awful fate of the son.

We have an addition to our works on Chemistry, in the treatise of Professor Johnson, of Yale College, entitled, How Plants Grow,—the Composition, Structure, and Life of the Plant. The illustrations and tables of analyses will aid the reader. Songs of the American Colleges (twenty-one colleges), with piano-forte accompaniment, will help in the social entertainment. The Life of George Stephenson and of his Son, in handsome octavo, with illustrations and portraits of these celebrated English Inventors, by Smiles, whose other works we have, will be found instructive, especially in their connection with the history of the invention and introduction of the Railway Locomotive. Sketches of Governor Andrew, by Browne, and the admirable Eulogy on his Life and Character, by Nason, have been added; also four separate treatises on General Grant, by Adams, Coppié, Moore, and Richardson; one on Colfax; and one each on Seymour and Blair. Warned by the numerous conventions and discussions in this country and abroad, for adjusting the position of woman in the social scale, your Trustees have hastened to place on the shelves these five volumes,—Friendships of Women, by Rev. William R. Alger; Celebrated Women; Modern Women; World-Noted Women; Eminent

Women. Few handsomer books have gone there during the year. And certainly these grand portraits, these grander lives, for beauty and true nobility of soul make good their claim to all the "Rights" which man has to bestow.

Histories of many of our modern military regiments have been published; but rare, indeed, have been works like one which we have added the past year, History of the First New Hampshire, in the War of the Revolution, by Frederic Kidder. Among the first organized, soon after the battle of Lexington, it was about the longest in the field, disbanded at the close of 1783. Names of its four commanding officers, Stark, Cilley, Scammell, Dearborn, and of its privates, in all more than a thousand, whose descendants are widely scattered, are given, with residences, enlistments, fortunes, deaths, — a most engaging volume. Of local, town, and city histories, we have added between thirty and forty to our collection, which embraces that of Pittsfield, just from the press; Hudson's valuable History of Lexington, likewise lately printed, and his earlier History of Marlboro'; Histories of Boston, by Drake, Quincy, Sumner, and Bowen; Bond's Watertown; Shattuck's Concord; Caleb Butler's Groton; Cowley's Lowell; Ricketson's New Bedford; Washburn's Leicester; the History of Duxbury, by Justin Winsor, the accomplished Superintendent of the Boston Public Library; Sewall's Woburn; Whitney's History of the Several Towns in Worcester County; Mitchell's Bridgewater; Jackson's Newton; Abbott's Andover; Sibley's Union, Maine; the exhaustive works of Felt and Upham on Salem, and Felt's History of Ipswich. Of New York, we have Irving's History; Barber's Historical Collections; Smith's Sunshine and Shadow; and the Great Metropolis, by Browne. Historical Collections of the Several States, by Barber and by Howe; Early Recollections of Newport, by George G. Channing; Histories of Lynn, by Lewis and by Newhall; of Newbury, by Coffin; of Montpelier, Vermont; of Windsor, Connecticut; of Mason,

New Hampshire; of Norway, Maine, and of various other towns, cities, and states are likewise comprised.

Cary's Translation of Dante; Home Pictures of English Poets; a volume of Poems, by Lucy Larcom, which the high judgment of Whittier commends; Longfellow's New England Tragedies, and the last poetical contributions of Lowell and of Whittier (Under the Willows, and Among the Hills) — have been added. Darley's Sketches Abroad with Pen and Pencil, is a rare collection of gems. American Note-Books, in two volumes, by our gifted Hawthorne, lately deceased, of whom the "London Spectator" says, "We doubt if any English writer living writes so pure and classical English," is now added to all the author's previous works in the Library, and will hold the reader's interest to the end, as with the grasp of a genius. Life and Letters of Fitz Greene Halleck, by his friend and literary executor, General James Grant Wilson, with a portrait of the poet, and view of his residence and monument at Guilford, Connecticut, his birthplace, will not wait long for readers. But fifteen months have gone over the yet green grave of one of the most gifted and genial of American poets, whose private life and manners and conversation were as sweet as his verse. For his worth of character, for the affection which he inspired, for his merits as a poet and a man, we recall few writers who have won such commendation from worthiest authorities. Few American poets have been more read in our homes, and we gladly place this choice volume by the side of his poems in the library. His "Marco Bozzaris," familiar to our school boys, is pronounced by some critics, the best martial lyric in the English tongue. Wider than in any other of his verses, is he probably known in those touching lines in which he mourned his chosen friend and literary colleague, Joseph Rodman Drake, who died in 1820. Though often quoted they have not seldom been misquoted; and we here write, them once more, alike in memory of their cherished author and as a fit close to this brief nomenclature of accomplished men and women; some once his associates below; some with him now above, and all kindred in the spiritual ties of reason and imagination, of fancy and feeling which forever connect the wise and good, the teachers and guides of their race :—

> "Green be the turf above thee, —
> Friend of my better days;
> None knew thee but to love thee,
> Nor named thee but to praise."

We have thus briefly mentioned nearly two hundred volumes from among the whole collection added during the past year, and, like all added since June, 1866, not contained on the printed catalogues. They may represent classes, in which those books not named would rank. We have put in six hundred volumes in the twelve months. This seems a very small addition when contrasted with the eighty-three hundred which the magnificent Boston Library put in during the year. But appearances are sometimes deceitful. Which library really added the most? Recall that incident on which, eighteen hundred years ago, the Master, "as he sat over against the treasury" in Jerusalem, pronounced judgment, while "all the people were very attentive to hear him." The "two mites which make a farthing," and the Roman talents of gold, were the theme; and Christianity and the gospel are not so far outgrown yet, but that a grateful world reads it today with admiration. It was, after all, a matter of ratios and proportions; and we may again state it on this wise. If a small municipality of five thousand inhabitants adds in a year to its public library six hundred volumes, how many volumes should a municipality of two hundred and fifty thousand inhabitants add? Why, as the latter municipality is fifty times larger than the former, it should add, to be equal in ratio, fifty times as many books, or fifty times six hundred, which is thirty thousand. But the good old municipality, her exact library-superintendent tells us, added eight thousand three hundred. Did not, then, the small municipality "cast in more than they all"? Nay, reverse this proportion, and state it thus: if a municipality of two hundred and fifty thousand inhabitants adds in a year to its public library eight thousand three hundred books, how many books, to be equal in ratio, should a municipality of five thousand inhabitants add? One fiftieth part of eight thousand, three hundred books, the bright primary-school scholar will tell us, — or exactly one hundred and sixty-six books. The small municipality, then, added nearly four times as many books as the large municipality, in proportion.

May the Library with which we are put in trust continue still to share the interest of our citizens. Books, — what power, what charms, what real life abides in them and goes out from them! Power, — for how books more than armies have overturned empires hoary with age, and perhaps with ignorance and wrong! Charms, — for who can fitly tell the satisfaction and joy of good books? Life, — for do not good books nourish the true life of the soul? Yes, next to food, raiment, shelter, we all want them. Architecture adds, each day, to her triumphs in elegant mansions all about us for human habitations. Why will we not all say that so shall rise a comely and fair-proportioned edifice for these books; that each year, multiplied, they may pass safely into the hands of those who shall come after us, — nay, that in the wisdom they may impart, in the good principles they may help establish in the hearts of this generation, they may continue to live in the generations to come?

On page 9 of this Report allusion is made to the excellent hymn, in connection with its author, which was sung on the occasion of laying the corner-stone of the new library edifice at Newton. With three stanzas of this hymn, so true and beautiful, which have specially no local application, the gifted poet must suffer us to conclude this communication: —

> "'Tis not by earthly bread alone
>   That man, the immortal, moves and lives;
> And what is life without the charm
>   Which gentle Christian culture gives?
>
> "In vain these fair and stately homes,
>   Though decked in wealth and pride of art,
> Without the treasures of the mind,
>   And choicer treasures of the heart!
>
> "So build we here a house for thought,
>   Which after-time shall guard and keep;
> For generations yet unborn
>   We lay foundations strong and deep."

Respectfully submitted,
In behalf of the Trustees,

FREDERIC A. WHITNEY,
President.

WILLIAM WIRT WARREN,
CHARLES HENRY BASS BRECK,
GRANVILLE FULLER,
JOHN PERKINS CUSHING WINSHIP.

EDMUND RICE,
LIFE BALDWIN, *Treasurer,*
WLLIAM FREDERIC MATCHETT,
BELA STODDARD FISKE, *Secretary.*

FREDERIC AUGUSTUS WHITNEY,
WEARE DOW BICKFORD,
WEBSTER FRANKLIN WARREN, *Librarian.*
NATHANIEL JACKSON.

Trustees by triennial, biennial, and annual election.

HOLTON LIBRARY, January 30, 1869.

REPORT

OF THE

LIBRARIAN OF THE HOLTON LIBRARY.

To THE TRUSTEES:

The Librarian herewith submits the fifth Annual Report for the year ending January 31, 1869.

The Library is at present in the following condition: —

Number of volumes belonging to the Library at the commencement of the year,	4,421
Number of volumes added by purchase, and by binding periodicals,	539
Number of volumes presented,	66
	5,026
Number of volumes purchased to supply the places of books worn out or defaced,	18
Total number of volumes February 1, 1869,	5,008
Number of pamphlets February 1, 1868,	689
" added by purchase,	376
" " presentation,	120
Total number of pamphlets added to February 1, 1869,	1,185
Number of subscribers February 1, 1868,	1,349
" " for the past year,	210
Total number " since the opening of the Library in 1864,	1,559

Number of subscribers who have taken out books during the past year, ... 950
Number of books taken out during the year, . 17,303
Average number taken by each subscriber, . . 18
Number of days (including evenings) on which the Library has been open, ... 92
Average number taken out each day, . . . 188

Amount expended for books, periodicals, and stationery, ... $1,182 12
Amount received from fines, ... $50 66

PERIODICALS.

Atlantic Monthly.	Harper's Weekly.
Cornhill Magazine.	Leslie's Magazine.
Eclectic Magazine.	Littell's Living Age.
Every Saturday.	North American Review.
Galaxy.	Our Young Folks' Magazine.
Genealogical Register.	Punch.
Godey's Magazine.	Scientific American.
Harper's Magazine.	The Horticulturist.

The usual annual examination of the Library was made in August last, showing a loss, since the former report, of four books, namely, "Volume II. of Charles Dickens's works," "Paul Ferrol," "Can You Forgive Her?" and "The Life of Admiral Farragut." Two of these books were charged to subscribers. In one instance we were unable to find the subscriber at the place given by him as his residence, and have not yet been able to find any such person, though a careful search has been made through the street where he stated his residence to be at the time of his application. In the other case it appeared that the card had been used by some person unknown to the subscriber. On applying to the person who should have had the book, we could learn nothing in regard to it. The last Boston Report, on page 46, cites cases very similar to this. The volume of Dickens's works is the most valuable of the missing books, as it formed one of a series of five volumes containing nearly all the works of that author, and the difficulty of replacing it will be far greater than obtaining new copies of the other books, which are complete in themselves. In other forms all of Dickens's works are contained in the Library. It is possible that some of these volumes may be in the possession of persons who have unintentionally neglected to return them. If any one can give information which will enable us to recover any lost volumes, we shall be well pleased to receive it, as it is very desirable to reduce the absolute losses to the smallest possible number. They may wander home. It is stated that twenty-four volumes, reported missing from the Boston Athenæum in 1866, have reappeared.

The total number of volumes loaned is somewhat smaller than during the previous year. This may be partly explained from the fact that during the former year no intermission was taken for an examination; while during the month of August and a part of September of the last year no books were delivered from the Library. The number of books delivered shows a larger average for each day than in the previons year; but the increase is not so great as the larger number of users and the additional number of books would seem to warrant. With our present number of volumes and subscribers, we should have delivered from two to three thousand more books than we actually did in order to have our circulation equivalent to that of last year. The difficulty of obtaining the more popular works of fiction has been such, that cards on which ten or even twenty numbers were written have frequently been returned to subscribers for the insertion of more numbers, none of the books first called for being in the Library. The number of duplicates now proposed to be added, with the addition hereafter of duplicate copies of such works as may be deemed necessary, will partially remedy this annoyance. The additional aid of a printed supplement will undoubtedly greatly increase the use of such works as have been added since the printing of the Catalogue in 1866.

As is shown by the statement in the first part of this Report, we have added more than six hundred books during the past year, of which about one-third are works of fiction; making the whole number belonging to the Library at the close of the past year somewhat over five thousand volumes. No duplicates have as yet been procured, except in the case of the works of "L. Muhlbach," mentioned in the former Report; but it is proposed to immediately duplicate the works of several of the more prominent authors of fiction, as the demand for those works, as in most other public libraries, is far greater than we are able to meet with our present supply.

It becoming apparent during the year that our shelf-room, at our present rate of increase, would be very soon taken up, it was found necessary to extend the shelving; and, during the month of August, while the Library was closed for the examination, six new alcoves were arranged, furnishing us sufficient room for two thousand volumes. No more shelf-room can be well supplied in the hall; and, with the present liberal means furnished for procuring books, our increase in the coming years will be much greater than in the past. The want of a commodious building, to be devoted to the Library alone, becomes continually more apparent.

The attention of the Trustees is again called to the necessity of a printed supplement. Between eleven and twelve hundred books, or nearly a quarter of the whole number belonging to the Library, including all the later novels, have been added since the Catalogue was printed. The titles of added books are immediately written in a few catalogues at the Library. Still, as those catalogues can only be consulted at the Library, they are of little value to the large number of subscribers who seldom visit the hall, but send their cards by other persons. The number of written supplements is necessarily so small in proportion to the card-holders, as to render the task of selecting a book at the Library rather inconvenient.

The Reading Room has been resorted to by more people than in former years, and the magazines to be found there are receiving more attention each year. The demand for books of reference to be consulted at the Library has been very small, — so small as to induce the belief that many of our citizens do not know that there are a large number of volumes, too valuable for general circulation, which may be examined there on any afternoon or evening when books are delivered. No alteration has been made in the list of magazines since the Report of last year. The inquiry has sometimes been made whether the Reading Room would not be of more benefit if subscribers could have access to it more frequently than they may under our present arrangement. Whether the extra use that would be made of the room if it was available on more days would justify the additional expense, is of course a question to be decided by the Trustees.

The order observed both in the hall of delivery, and in the Reading Room has been generally good. Still, as the design of the Reading Room does not seem to be fully comprehended by a portion of our subscribers, it may not be out of place to state here, that all selections of books, or consultations of catalogues, and all inquiries as to books, are expected to be made in the front hall. It is impossible, by any other course, to secure the stillness requisite to enable readers to make either a pleasant, or profitable use of the Reading Room. A still greater hindrance to the comfortable use of the Reading Room is the very uncomfortable habit, existing to some extent, of making that a room for social conversation. This evil is not indulged in so much as formerly; and it would seem as if a moment's reflection would convince offenders that a proper regard for the rights and comforts of others required them to abstain from a practice so disagreeable to all who resort to the room to read.

The general treatment of books loaned has been as good

as can be reasonably expected. The larger portion of the volumes purchased to supply those worn out have filled the places of books which were formerly in use in the Brighton Library Association and have been in constant circulation since they were made a part of the present Library. In some cases these earlier books have been abused; but in nearly all instances the books are actually worn out, having been bound so many times that, in trimming the edges of the leaves, a portion of the printed matter is clipped for a number of pages, making it very difficult for a reader to learn what the original words were. It is gratifying to know that the books so lost are usually such as can readily be replaced, — being generally of the class called for by the younger readers, and being in such demand that new copies can always can be procured.

Appended is a list of donors for the past year with the number of volumes and pamphlets presented by each.

All of which is respectfully submitted,

W. F. WARREN, *Librarian.*

HOLTON LIBRARY, Jan. 31, 1869.

BENEFACTORS

TO THE

HOLTON LIBRARY,

FOR THE YEAR 1868-9.

And the Number of Volumes and Pamphlets received from each.

JAMES HOLTON'S ORIGINAL BEQUEST . . $6,000.

Names and Residence.	Pamphlets.	Vols.
Baxter, Daniel, Brighton	–	1
Boston Public Library, Trustees of	2	–
Boutwell, George S., Hon., Washington, D. C.	22	40
Bradlee, Caleb Davis, Rev., Boston	3	–
Champney, William Richards, Brighton	2	
Manchester Public Library, Trustees of	7	–
Massachusetts, Commonwealth of		6
Matchett, William Frederic, Brighton	–	1
Niles, Thomas, Brighton	2	–
Peabody Institute, Trustees of, Peabody	2	–
Rice, Abigail, Mrs., Brighton	1	1
Rice, Edmund, Brighton	–	2
Sumner, Charles, Hon., Washington, D. C.	1	
Tyler, John S., Mrs., Boston	76	7
Whitney, Augustus Anson, Cambridge	–	1
Whitney, Frederic A., Rev., Brighton	1	1
Whitney, Frederic A., Mrs., Brighton	–	1
Winship, J. P. C., Brighton	–	5
Worcester Public Library, Directors of	1	–
	120	66

TREASURER'S REPORT.

Life Baldwin, Treasurer, in account with Holton Library.

Dr.

1868.				
Feb.		To balance of funds on hand,	$4,578 31	
May	7.	" cash of Librarian, for fines, to May 1, 1868,	11 96	
July	1.	" cash one year's interest on $3,800 U. S. Bonds, $228, prem. $91 20,	319 20	
Aug.	21.	" cash of Librarian, fines for 3 months, to Aug. 1, 1868,	19 77	
Nov.	18.	" cash of Librarian, fines for 3 months ending Nov. 1, 1868,	7 47	
1869.				
Jan.	1.	" cash six months' interest on $3,800 U. S. Bonds, $114, prem. $39 33,	153 33	
Feb.	4.	" cash of Librarian, fines 3 months ending Feb. 1, 1869,	11 46	
	4.	" cash H. H. Learnard, Treasurer, Town appropriation for 1868,	500 00	
				$5,601 50

Cr.

1868.			
Feb.	29.	By cash paid J. O. Tubbs, setting glass, &c.,	$1 75
March 19.		" cash paid Flint Brothers, account,	7 20
	19.	" cash paid Nichols & Noyes, books,	56 12
		Amount carried forward,	$65 07

Amount brought forward,		$65 07
March 27. By cash paid Sweetser & Abbott, carpet, &c.,		22 24
April 10. " cash paid W. F. Warren, Geo. Fisher's bill,		8 50
10. " cash paid Hooper, Lewis, & Co., paper, &c.,		82 70
15. " cash paid Nichols & Noyes, books,		56 41
May 7. " cash paid W. F. Warren, sundries,		7 96
15. " cash paid Nichols & Noyes, books,		27 41
July 16. " cash paid W. F. Warren (W. B. Towne's bill),		1 50
16. " cash paid W. F. Warren, Life of Grant,		1 50
16. " cash paid Nichols & Noyes, books,		128 19
16. " cash paid S. G. Drake, books,		20 50
16. " " Crosby & Ainsworth, books,		70 85
16. " cash paid W. H. Piper, books,		41 25
Aug. 21. " " W. F. Warren, sundries,		9 77
22. " cash paid Nichols & Noyes, books,		91 24
Oct. 16. " cash paid Nichols & Noyes, books,		161 05
16. " cash paid Hooper, Lewis, & Co., books,		8 00
Nov. 18. " cash paid W. F. Warren, sundries,		5 13
Dec. 2. " cash paid W. S. Bartlett, books,		15 98
2. " " Nichols & Noyes, books,		98 08
18. " cash paid Nichols & Noyes, books,		72 76
Amount carried forward,		$996 09

	Amount brought forward,	$996 09	
1869.			
Feb.	4. By cash paid A. Williams & Co., books,	68 30	
	4. " cash paid Hooper, Lewis, & Co., paper,	1 75	
	4. " cash paid Nichols & Noyes, books,	73 73	
	4. " cash paid Nichols & Noyes, books,	65 72	
	4. " cash paid W. F. Warren, sundries,	7 72	
	6. " balance on hand in U. S. Bonds, $3,800; cash in Bank, $588 19,	4,388 19	
			$5,601 50

Respectfully submitted by

L. BALDWIN, *Treasurer.*

HOLTON LIBRARY, Feb. 6, 1869.

HOLTON LIBRARY, Feb. 11, 1869.

The undersigned, appointed to audit the accounts of the Treasurer, for the past year, has examined the same, and finds them correctly kept, and properly vouched; and a balance in the hands of the Treasurer of three thousand and eight hundred dollars ($3,800) in United States bonds, and five hundred and eighty-eight dollars and nineteen cents ($588.19) in cash.

(Attest) B. S. FISKE, *Auditor.*

APPENDIX.

BOOKS OF REFERENCE.

ALLUSION is made, on page thirty-seven and on page twenty-three of the library reports, to the books of reference comprised in the collection. The Pictorial History of the Great Rebellion, spoken of on page twenty-three, as embraced in two large folio volumes, a most complete and reliable narrative of the war, contains *one thousand* illustrations, not simply *one hundred*, as the oft-erring types have, in this instance, signified. These illustrations embrace a great variety of scenes and incidents in the war, — as we count them, between five and six hundred pictures. Then of maps and plans, without which the campaigns and contests cannot be well comprehended, there are ninety-seven. Of portraits of those who served in the war, on both sides, there are between three and four hundred. The valuable work on Mines and Miners is particularly described on page seven. Included likewise, among the books of reference, are the various cyclopædias and dictionaries and magazines, American and foreign, as designated on the catalogues and supplements by an asterisk (*). Allibone's large dictionary of Authors and English Literature, of which the second volume is soon expected from the press, and Eschenburg's Classical Manual of Literature are here comprised.

The Numismatical Manual, by Dickeson, elegantly illustrated with specimens of gold, silver, and copper coins, attracts notice. It contains, moreover, engravings of the wampum or money of the aborigines of America, with the colonial, State, and United States coins. These illustrations are made more valuable, as accurate historical and descriptive notices of each coin or series are added. The same subject is treated in another volume of reference, entitled Coins, Medals, and Seals, and partially in the attractive work, Medallic Memorial of Washington. Chapel and Church Architecture; Pilgrims of Boston, by Bridgman; Plans of Bunker Hill Monument; Catalogues of various Public Libraries; Colton's General Atlas; Eighty Years' Progress, speaking to the eye, as well as to the mind; The Family Farm and Garden; Information for the People, by Chambers; Punch, the entertaining, and Gleason's Pictorial, — will be found here. Hitchcock's Geology of Mass., and his Ichnology of New England; Natural History of Birds, Reptiles, Fishes, by Wood, copiously illustrated; Agassiz' Natural History of the United States, in four volumes; Nature Displayed, by Dufief, in two volumes; the four large works from the French, of Louis Figuier, named on page twenty-five; and Cloud Crystals, richly and delicately painted, deserve mention. And we may still add from the many left unnamed, The Scientific American, in several volumes; Reports of the Smithsonian Institute, and various other valuable Congressional and Public reports; Moore's Records of the Rebellion, in eleven volumes, and Lossing's Field Book of the Revolution, in two volumes.

All volumes of reference may be examined and read at the tables, on every day and evening when the Library is open, on application to the Librarian. Card-holders have also the privilege of reading at the hall any volume on the shelves, observing the regulation which forbids conversation here. They must, moreover, be held responsible for the return of the books, thus consulted, to the attendant before leaving the hall. The Trustees desire certainly that the books may serve the greatest number of readers possible, consistent with the due care and preservation of such as are especially valuable, or in any way restricted by the terms of bequest. They have accordingly left many books to be lent from the hall, which, perhaps, from their many illustrations, would in other public libraries have been designated as books of reference.

As these previous sheets of the Library Reports have just come from the press, a few typographical errors, such as often elude the utmost care, may be here corrected. On page 7, line 2, from the bottom, "minerals" should be "animals." On page 24, line 12, from the bottom, the word "entertaining," not satisfied with the letter t, rightfully belonging to it twice, must needs take it a third time; while, in the same line, the little word "it" is cheated out of its apostrophe and s. On page 25, line 10, Dr. Bushnell's name may be amended; and in line 6 from the bottom, the learned Swedish Professor would ask that the "i" be stricken out from the city of his University. In the last word of the next line, the reader's eye will detect the error; while, on page 28, line 5 from the bottom, so simple a thing as substituting a period for a semi-colon, as the copy had it, will be the salvation of the grammar. On page 30, line nineteen, "on" must be substituted for "in." On page 34, line 5 from the bottom, an s is unnecessarily absent; and lastly, on page 36, line 10, the L, in the name of the fine authoress, Louisa Muhlbach, has been Frenchified into Le.

SIXTH ANNUAL REPORT

OF THE

TRUSTEES

OF THE

HOLTON LIBRARY,

BRIGHTON.

SIXTH ANNUAL REPORT

OF THE

TRUSTEES

OF THE

HOLTON LIBRARY,

BRIGHTON,

FEBRUARY 1, 1870.

BOSTON:
ROCKWELL & CHURCHILL, PRINTERS,
122 WASHINGTON STREET.
1870.

TOWN OF BRIGHTON.

HOLTON LIBRARY, Feb. 1, 1870.

TO THE AUDITORS:

Gentlemen: — I have the honor to transmit to you, herewith, the Sixth Annual Report of the Trustees of the Holton Library, prepared in obedience to the Ordinance adopted by the Town, April 8, 1864.

Yours respectfully,

B. S. FISKE,
Secretary of the Board of Trustees.

TRUSTEES

Of the Library from its Commencement.

BALDWIN, LIFE	1864
BENYON, ABNER INGALLS	1866–68
BICKFORD, WEARE DOW	1864
BRECK, CHARLES HENRY BASS	1867
CUSHMAN, JOHN PAINE	1864–66
FISKE, BELA STODDARD	1865
FULLER, GRANVILLE	1864
HUTCHINSON, CHARLES CARROLL	1864–65
JACKSON, NATHANIEL	1864–69
MATCHETT, THEODORE	1864–67
MATCHETT, WILLIAM FREDERIC	1867
PACKARD, DAVID TURNER	1869
POND, JOSEPH ADAMS	1864–67
RICE, EDMUND	1865
RUGGLES, JOHN	1864–65
WARREN, WEBSTER FRANKLIN	1869
WARREN, WILLIAM WIRT	1864
WHITNEY, FREDERIC AUGUSTUS	1864
WINSHIP, JOHN PERKINS CUSHING	1864

OFFICERS

Of the Library from its Commencement.

PRESIDENTS.

JOHN RUGGLES,	April 18, 1864 — October 9, 1865.
FREDERIC AUGUSTUS WHITNEY,	November 13, 1865 —

SECRETARIES.

JOHN PERKINS CUSHING WINSHIP,	April 18, 1864 — March 13, 1865.
BELA STODDARD FISKE,	March 13, 1865 —

TREASURER.

LIFE BALDWIN,	May 23, 1864 —

LIBRARIANS.

JOHN PERKINS CUSHING WINSHIP,	June 13, 1864 — July 9, 1866.
WEBSTER FRANKLIN WARREN,	July 9, 1866 —

SIXTH ANNUAL REPORT

OF THE

TRUSTEES OF THE HOLTON LIBRARY.

IN obedience to the Ordinance respecting the Holton Library, adopted by the Town of Brighton, April 8, 1864, the Trustees have the honor to submit their Sixth Annual

REPORT.

They are not called to report on a subject foreign to the thoughts and interests of their fellow-citizens. The privileges of the Public Library have become with these successive years so generally known and shared in the homes of the people; the institution is so peculiarly their own; — an institution, to use the words of the lamented Lincoln, in a different application, "of the people, by the people, for the people," — that their report to us, not ours to them, might seem more fit.

I. THE PEOPLE'S REPORT.

The people do report. And if ever in any tone of fault-finding, it cannot be, we are sure, with the beneficent institution itself, but rather with their servants' faulty administration of this grand trust. The people do report their very great satisfaction that they possess a Public Library. They do report, and to some fresh page of their report we open weekly, that it is well, a blessing among the greatest, that so many books for entertainment and instruction are presented them without money and without price. They do report satisfaction that books of their own choice, which the Library Committee may perchance have overlooked, they can still have placed on the shelves for the asking. They have reported, and not unfavorably, certainly with another year, in the calls they have made in these twelve months, for the delivery of more than fifteen thousand volumes, to be taken to their homes; for so say the Librarian's returns.

II. ADMINISTRATION OF THE PAST YEAR.

But certain items of information touching the Library, the citizens rightly expect shall be, each year, laid before them, and such deficiencies and wants stated, as they can remedy and supply, and thereby increase the usefulness of the institution. At the annual town meeting, in March, 1869, four of the Trustees, one class, Messrs. Whitney, Bickford, Warren (Webster Franklin), and Jackson, whose term of office then expired, were re-elected for three years. At the approaching town meeting, March, 1870, the term of office of Messrs. Rice, Baldwin, Matchett, and Fiske will expire, and the town will be called to elect. At the monthly meeting of the Board of Trustees, held April 12th, Mr. Jackson, who had served since the establishment of the Library, tendered his resignation; and Rev. David Turner Packard was chosen in his place. The officers of the previous year, President, Secretary, Treasurer, and Librarian, were re-elected for the service of 1869-70. The two assistants of the Librarian, Frederic Augustus Pierce and Hiram Norton Cushman, who had been employed two years, while advanced scholars in the High School, were retained until June last. Subsequently, Henry Warren, son of Noah Warren Sanborn, of this town; George Hartwell, son of the late Samuel Hartwell

Moore, of Worcester, and Herbert Langdon, son of the late Joseph Langdon Waterman, of this town, were engaged, of whom the latter two are still in service.

III. FINANCES.

By the Sixth Annual Report of the Treasurer, Mr. Baldwin, which accompanies this Report, it will be seen that a portion of the principal of the liberal bequest of Mr. Holton, the founder, has been expended during the past year. This is understood to be in conformity with the legal requisitions of his legacy. The town, as usual, made an appropriation towards the support of the Library, at their last annual meeting. It will appear that more has been expended for books than in most previous years. The expenses of the Library, it will be remembered, are drawn from two treasuries. The Treasurer of the Board of Trustees meets all demands for books, paper, and sundries for the Library, when regularly vouched by the President and Secretary; while the salary of the Librarian, including the pay of the assistants, the charges for repairs on the building, for gas and coal, are drawn from the town treasury. On these conditions, the town accepted the original legacy.

IV. LIBRARIAN'S REPORT.

The Librarian, being now a member of the Board of Trustees, presents in his Report only the statistics pertaining to the Library. Such suggestions as have, hitherto, been expected in that document, are now presented at the monthly meetings. It will be seen that he records as the number of volumes belonging to the Library, on the first day of February, 1870, five-thousand eight hundred and thirty-eight. Of pamphlets, there are one thousand six hundred and seventy-seven. In this last enumeration are comprised periodicals, reviews, and magazines, both such as from time to time are donated, and such as are received by subscription for the tables of the Reading Room. These latter, of course, at the close of each year, when sets are completed, are bound and are placed upon the shelves. Fifty-six volumes, and one hundred and sixteen pamphlets, the Librarian reports presented during the past year.

V. DONATIONS.

Donations in books and pamphlets, both from our own citizens and from abroad, have been continued as in past years. While we should have been glad to record on the list of donors' names of more of the inhabitants of the town, we are thankful for such as have thereby manifested interest in the institution. This kind of interest, it must be remembered, is, by no means, to be undervalued in comparison with the pecuniary estimate of the donations. A free Public Library, with but moderate pecuniary foundation, will more truly prosper in this encouraging favor of its patrons than the most amply endowed Library without it. We cannot but look with pride on the donations of books, — from single volumes to scores, from individuals of no wealth to millionnaires, — which flow each year into the Public Library of our good old metropolis. Larger has the stream been last year than ever before. The Annual Report of the Trustees, lately issued, has twelve closely printed pages of names of donors, six hundred and forty-nine in all, and states that of the entire increase of volumes last year, eight thousand six hundred and eighty-five, nearly one-quarter were given; and of the pamphlets, about fourteen thousand, nearly four-fifths were given.

The Hon. Secretary of the United States Treasury, Mr. Boutwell, our late Representative in Congress, has furnished some thirty Public Documents, thereby keeping sets complete, and adding much of permanent value to a Public Library. This liberality Mr. Boutwell has not omitted for a single year since the Library was founded. To the Rev.

Caleb Davis Bradlee of Boston, a frequent contributor before, we are indebted, with the past year, for a complete set of the Historical Magazine,—a recent publication, in nine volumes, quarto, very handsomely bound, the pecuniary value of which the Librarian estimates at some twenty-five or thirty dollars. This work embracing much information, with the valuable fruits of historical research, is distinct from the New England Historical and Genealogical Register, a very important quarterly publication, which we also possess, now entering upon its twenty-fourth volume. The School Committee of Boston have presented, through their Secretary, Mr. Barnard Capen, twelve volumes, bound, of their School Reports, towards completing our series. As our town will, beyond doubt, be very soon annexed to Boston, it is especially desirable that works of this class should be on the shelves of the Library, which will thus become a branch of the Public Library of the city.

To Mr. Joseph Lovell Bates, of Boston, Secretary of the Massachusetts Charitable Mechanic Association, we are also indebted for a complete set of the publications of that association, extending over a period of thirty-three years, from 1837, the date of its organization, to the present year. A complete account of each of the grand exhibitions of the Mechanic Association's Fairs, held at stated intervals, in Fanueil and Quincy Halls, Boston, is furnished, with the Report of the Board of Managers, the Report of the Judges, the prizes, medals, premiums awarded, together with the names of persons exhibiting articles, among whom several from our own town are recorded. This series of publications embraces likewise the Occasional Address delivered by some distinguished man, in each year of the grand exhibition. The first of these, as may be remembered, was the admirable discourse pronounced by Hon. Edward Everett, then Governor of the Commonwealth, on "The Importance of the Mechanic Arts." Others in the series, most instructive and entertaining, are from Hon. James T. Austin; Hon. Stephen

Fairbanks; Hon. George Lunt; Mr. Skinner, of Philadelphia, a Representative of the Editorial Staff, on "The Interests of American Labor;" by Mr. George Russell, on "The Achievements of American Mind and American Labor;" by Rev. Frederic D. Huntington, D.D., on "The Hands, Brain, Heart," which was afterwards repeated in the regular winter course of lectures, in our Town Hall, 1856; by Hon. Emory Washburn, Law Professor, in Harvard University, on "The Relation of the Mechanic Arts to the Social and Political Condition of the World;" by Hon. Alexander H. Bullock, Governor, on "The Mechanic Arts favorable to Liberty and Social Progress." The perusal of these all is most highly commended now, especially, for incitement and encouragement, to such as are engaged in the Mechanic Arts.

Mr. Life Baldwin of this town, while member of the House of Representatives in the last Legislature, has kindly supplied us with State documents. Mr. Richard Cranch Greenleaf of Boston, one of the Board of Directors of the Home for Aged Men, has presented his last Annual Report, with a complete set of the reports of that beneficent institution since its establishment; and also three volumes, — an approved modern Treatise on the "Principles of Zoology," by Professor Agassiz and A. A. Gould; "History, Theory, and Practice of the Electric Telegraph," by George B. Prescott; "Biographical Guide to the Literature on Sciences," by L. M. Schmidt; together with some twenty-five pamphlets of interest. Mrs. Dwight Boyden Hooper of this town has given eleven volumes. The names of all donors of books will be found enumerated in the Librarian's Report, to each of whom he has returned the Trustees' acknowledgment of thanks in the customary printed form.

VI. A SPECIAL DONATION.

A valuable donation, entitled to special notice, has been recently made to the Library by Mrs. Matchett, of this town, of three hundred dollars, for the purchase of a clock. At the meeting of the Trustees in December last, Rev. Messrs. Packard and Whitney were appointed to prepare resolutions in acknowledgment of the gift. At the next regular meeting, January 10, 1870, the following Preamble and Resolutions were reported and unanimously adopted, and are here transcribed from the records: —

"Whereas, the Trustees of the Holton Library, at their regular meeting on the evening of December 13, 1869, were informed by their President, that Mrs. William Frederic Matchett, now passing the winter at the South for the benefit of her health, had, through him, presented to the Institution three hundred dollars, for the purchase of a clock for the inner Hall of the Library, therefore,

"*Resolved*, That the Trustees gratefully accept the generous gift, with pride that this largest donation since the original legacy of the founder has come to them from a native-born daughter of the town, whose father's name is, by a late liberal bequest, already associated with one of our finest school edifices.

"*Resolved*, That the thanks of the Trustees be returned to Mrs. Matchett for her handsome benefaction; and that they hereby pledge themselves to preserve with care, and to transmit to their successors, this valuable and beautiful appendage to the Library.

"*Resolved*, That the Trustees, in conveying to Mrs. Matchett their grateful sense of her favor, take occasion to express their warmest wishes for the complete establishment of her health, and for her return in safety to her northern home.

"*Resolved*, That these Resolutions be entered on our Records, and that the Secretary transmit a copy of the same to Mrs. Matchett."

VII. GENEROSITY IN THE INTEREST OF PUBLIC LIBRARIES.

The last few years have been distinguished, in our own country certainly, by remarkable liberality on the part of individuals and communities in favor of public libraries. The Trustees, in their last Report, made mention of the recent benefactions of private citizens, and of the large appropriations of towns in this great interest. The unprecedented gifts of Mr. George Peabody; the bequest of Mr. Heard of Ipswich, of fifty thousand dollars; of Mr. Edmunds of Newton, of fifteen thousand; of Mr. Pratt of Lynn, of ten thousand, and the gifts of other generous men in Newton and in Watertown, and of the large town appropriation of Brookline, all in aid of library buildings and books, were detailed. And now, to this former encouraging intelligence, we cannot forbear adding some instances of similar generosity that have marked the year 1869. In the town of Washington, New Hampshire, a lady, Miss Sarah Shed, has, by a bequest, of which we are not informed, founded a Public Library. In Hingham, Massachusetts, one of her most liberal-hearted sons, Hon. Albert Fearing, whose name has become almost synonymous with noble-giving, so frequently has he thus befriended deserving causes and good institutions, has himself both furnished a building and endowed a library. The anniversary of national independence was, last summer, made doubly inspiring to the patriotic citizens of that ancient town by the dedicatory exercises of their Public Library. A very handsome wooden edifice, forty-five feet by twenty-eight, of peculiar and striking architecture, of two stories in height of twelve and fifteen feet, surmounted by a French roof, with all needed and spacious apartments, designed by Mr. Nathaniel J. Bradlee, was, by deed of conveyance from Mr. Fearing, presented to the town, on that anniversary, in an appropriate speech by the donor, to which a fitting reply was made by the President of the Trustees, Hon. Solomon Lincoln. Rev. Calvin Lincoln, of the First Church, offered the Prayer of Dedication, and Hon. Thomas Russell of Boston, delivered an eloquent oration. The items of expenditure, as we are informed, were, for land, one thousand five hundred and fifty dollars; for the building, twelve thousand dollars; for furniture, insurance, etc., one thousand four hundred and fifty dollars, making fifteen thousand dollars, to which was added an endowment-fund of five thousand dollars,— in all, twenty thousand dollars thus nobly appropriated by Mr. Fearing.

And yet another instance from the Empire State waits to be noticed, — the munificent donation just made, of Mr. James Lenox of New York City, for a free Public Library there. He conveys land to the Trustees of the Lenox Library, as a free gift to the city, between Seventy-second and Seventy-sixth Streets, opposite the Park, as a site for the edifice, and gives three hundred thousand dollars, or "any larger sum that may be needed to erect it." He covenants, moreover (we use the language of official documents), to transfer to the Trustees his entire collection of Statuary, Paintings, and Books, as a beginning for the library, and promises that no further sums of money shall be withheld that may be demanded to make this the finest Public Library in the country.

And this all is the benevolent work of one large-hearted man in the widest interest of humanity. This much he does in his lifetime, that books may be supplied to the public; that the poor as well as the rich may read; that all who will may inform themselves, without cost, in the current literature of their own time, and as they seek it, of all past ages. Would that the winds of heaven might waft the record of these generous deeds far and wide over the habitable globe!

VIII. INCREASE OF LIBRARIES.

As a natural result of this growing liberality towards Public Libraries, these beneficent institutions are rapidly increasing both in our own country and abroad. The last Report of the Superintendent of the Boston Public Library, Mr. Justin Winsor, appended to the Trustees' Report, especially confirms this. In Mr. Winsor's Report, which is really a marvel of careful labor and patient investigation, are given numerous tables, in which is most diligently arranged statistical information from the libraries of Massachusetts; secondly, other tables embracing similar information from libraries in the United States (Massachusetts excepted), and in British America; thirdly, tables with the statistics of libraries in England and Continental Europe. Our fellow-citizens, we are sure, will be pleased to learn, in connection with their own Library, something of the condition of similar institutions at home and abroad; and will be as ready as we to express their thanks to him who, with no little labor, has gathered so much information not otherwise accessible.

IX. LIBRARIES IN MASSACHUSETTS.

In these tables relating to Massachusetts, eighty-eight libraries are enumerated,—all that have made returns to Mr. Winsor at Boston, but not quite all in the State. In these are included the libraries of Colleges and Theological Institutions and various Associations, but nearly all are public town or city libraries. Private libraries of individuals are not included. Printed circulars were sent by the Superintendent to these libraries. They embraced thirty questions, such as these: When established? Income, and from what sources? Number of volumes and pamphlets? Average yearly increase for three years past? What proportion in fiction, and what in use of the same? Number of persons using the Library? Pecuniary guaranties, or vouchers required from borrowers? Books lost? Worn out? Donations? Have you printed catalogues? Reading Room for periodicals? Printed Reports? How many employed in Library? Books covered? Sell duplicates? How often do you buy particular books asked for by your frequenters? Library opened evenings? When closed for examination? Ages of your frequenters? System of charging and delivering books? How freely do you buy duplicates of popular works? etc., etc.

It is interesting to run the eye over the replies to these questions, so conveniently are they arranged in the tables above referred to. The admirable Report of Mr. Winsor may be found in our Library, with the entire series of reports from the Boston Library since its founding, in 1852. Of all the libraries named in Massachusetts, that returning the smallest number of volumes is at Rutland, lately opened, — three hundred and thirty-one books. The largest named in the tables is the Boston Public Library, — one hundred and fifty-three thousand. But this must properly be taken with one exception. The single exception is that of Harvard University. It is not uncommon in speaking of this, to enumerate only the library of the college proper, — that contained in Gore Hall, the Library edifice, and used by all undergraduates. But Harvard University has eight libraries kept in her other buildings, besides this portion in Gore Hall. The libraries of her Theological, Law, and Medical Colleges; the society libraries within the walls of the buildings which, not being private property, but, in part, the inheritance of past ages of the college, cannot be removed; the libraries of her Scientific School, her Observatory, her Botanical Garden, her Museum of Comparative Zoölogy, — all these collections of books are as truly parts of the University Library as that portion kept in Gore Hall. Thus they stand on the lately published annual catalogue of the University, as given in round numbers, up to July, 1869.

Library in Gore Hall,	121 000
Society Libraries of the University,	16 000
Library in Divinity College,	16 000
" " Medical "	2 000
" " Law "	15 000
" Museum of Comparative Zoology,	5 000
" Observatory (the Phillips),	3 000
" Botanical Garden,	3 000
" Lawrence Scientific School,	3 000
	184 000

The Library of Harvard University, thus enumerated, was accordingly the largest, not in Massachusetts, or the United States alone, but on the Western Continent, in July last.

During our late civil contest, with what interest we scanned the returns of army and military equipments, hospital stores, clothing and bandages furnished, and waiting in our small villages, our towns and cities, the hours of dreadful need! If, as Milton wrote so truly in his sonnet to Cromwell, —

" ———Peace hath her victories
No less renowned than war,"

shall we not, now that the din of battle has ceased, with a more tranquil and gladder satisfaction, contemplate the intellectual, moral, religious stores that are thus accumulating in all our towns, the preparations that are every year made therein, in commodious and well-ordered edifices and libraries, for the nobler victories of knowledge over ignorance for the most generous culture of the mind and heart.

The returns from Massachusetts libraries, in alphabetical order, arranged in distinct columns in tabular form, cover ten pages, octavo, of Mr. Winsor's Report. They relate to the year 1869, and of course may not quite agree with the condition of the same libraries to-day. Our own Library has been increased in books, and pamphlets in the binders hands, by nearly nine hundred volumes, since the returns in the tables were made. But, taking the numbers there given, and leaving out collegiate and city libraries, the number of volumes in our own Library was exceeded by only four in the Commonwealth; that of the Peabody Institute at Peabody, founded ten years before ours, and amply endowed by Mr. George Peabody; that of Brookline, seven years before; that of Fitchburg, five years, and that of Concord, thirteen years before. These tables afford easy opportunity for comparison in various other respects.

X. LIBRARIES IN THE UNITED STATES.

But not in the libraries of Massachusetts alone are we instructed, but ten pages more are filled with similar returns from the United States (Massachusetts excepted), and from British America. Seventy-five libraries are here reported in alphabetical order, of which the smallest consists of four hundred and eighty-two volumes, — the Wells Library, at Lee, Ohio, lately established; and the largest, the Washington Library of Congress, of one hundred and seventy-five thousand. The Astor and the Mercantile Libraries of New York city return one hundred and thirty-eight thousand, and one hundred and five thousand; the State Library at Albany, seventy-six thousand; Yale College, fifty thousand; the State Library at Harrisburg, Pa., thirty-nine thousand; Brown University, thirty-eight thousand; the Peabody Institute at Baltimore, thirty-five thousand. In British America, from among the six libraries making returns, the Parliament Library at Ottawa gives sixty thousand; and the Melbourne Public Library at Victoria, Australia, forty-seven thousand. And so by thousands, more or less, are all these beneficent collections, in our own land and near our borders, counted, — many of them freely thrown open, and all, more or less accessible to the public.

XI. LIBRARIES IN ENGLAND AND CONTINENTAL EUROPE.

And from England and Continental Europe have come statistical returns to the Superintendent at Boston. Indeed, so full and faithful a collection of the statistics of so many libraries of the world as he has given us has not before been made. The two largest free town-libraries returned from England are at Liverpool and at London, about eighty-seven thousand volumes each. No returns are given of the British Museum. We know it is unequalled in the world for its literary treasures and valuable relics of the past. The number of its volumes must be now nearly a million. The Royal City Library of Munich, founded before the year 1600, returns eight hundred thousand volumes. The Royal Library of Berlin, date 1662, seven hundred thousand. The recent Royal and University Library of Breslau, capital of Silesia, in Prussia, founded 1811–15, three hundred and sixty thousand. The Royal Library at Dresden, founded 1556, and the City Library, Hamburg, founded 1735, three hundred thousand each. The University Library, Upsala, Sweden, founded 1621, two hundred thousand. The information thus transmitted from these various sources will be found most valuable for comparison, and for the arrangement and management of our free Public Libraries. No less encouraging, moreover, is the wide view thus presented to all lovers of liberal culture and general dissemination of knowledge.

XI. EXAMINATION AND LOSSES.

The returns from all these libraries present no more convenient season for the annual examination of small libraries, than the month of August, which we have chosen. The Boston Public Library, indeed, has just adopted a new plan in this respect, and the last examination of the books has been made in sections, so that the library has not, at any season, been entirely closed to the public. It is said that this method has now, for the first time among all large libraries, been tried at Boston, and is much approved. Our patrons can best be deprived of the books in the debilitating heat of summer, and while so many are absent from their homes. Our ratio of losses is very small, either regarded absolutely, or relatively, as we compare the losses in other libraries in our own country and elsewhere.

XII. FINES.

The Treasurer's Report shows something added each year to the income from fines. The fine-system of course belongs to every public library that would retain its own existence. We do not wish, particularly, by means of fines, to add to the resources of the Library; but, obviously, delinquency in the return of books, must, like every other privilege, be paid for. By Article 5, Chapter II., of our printed Rules and Regulations, no book shall be kept out more than fourteen days, under penalty of five cents for each half week of such detention. One hundred and forty cards we are told were retained last year, at the Boston Public Library, for non-payment of fines, of which cards about half were subsequently settled for and returned. With the exception of new books in special demand, a volume, it must be remembered, may be renewed to the same borrower, and so the accident of fine be avoided.

XIII. DUPLICATES.

We have, perhaps, erred in not purchasing more duplicates the past year. Of some most popular works copies have been multiplied, but not of many. Managers of Public Libraries everywhere find this question of duplicates a vexed one. In Circulating Libraries it is easily solved. There, the rage for a popular work is at once and wisely improved as a means of enriching the treasury. Not a moment is lost, while the fever is at its height, for multiplying copies. The more copies, the more money in return; and when the fever is allayed, the extra copies are sold at auction. But free Public Libraries, without pecuniary returns for loans, must feel more carefully the public pulse, — must consider more diligently how high will rise this tide of popular favor; how soon, or suddenly, it will ebb. Books asked for, not already in the Library, we have in almost every instance procured; and the attention of the citizens is again called to the Record Book at the Librarian's desk, for recording their wishes in this particular. Not a single book, objectionable on moral grounds, has been entered on this Record since the Library was opened. The name of the person desiring a particular book is expected to be entered likewise. But on this whole matter of duplicates, and of books specially asked for, the inquiry is often made of us, "What is the usage elsewhere?" We can only refer to what we have said on this subject in former Reports, adding, this year, what Mr. Winsor has just given as one result from the inquiries proposed in his Circular. Thus, of the Massachusetts libraries, he writes:—

"In the purchase of books recommended, these libraries often, as far as they can, accede to any reasonable demand, — but in many cases no greater weight is given to a recommendation because a book is absolutely wanted, fitness in the Committee's eyes being the sole criterion. . . . The Boston Athenæum says, it buys on an average, three out of four that are recommended."

"In the purchase of duplicates, few of these libraries have means to satisfy the demands in this way. Some of them occasionally purchase two or three copies. . . . At the Boston Athenæum, they do not ordinarily duplicate in more than ten cases in a year; and the usage at the Boston Library Society is the same."

"I think the largest number of copies of a new book which has been bought the past year is seventeen, and this was in the case of 'The Gates Ajar.' As showing how libraries with different aims cater to such a demand, I will state that the Mercantile Library of New York, put fifty-two copies of that book in circulation; and that Mr. Loring of this city, found one hundred and fifty copies necessary to supply his customers." [A Circulating Library.]

The usage abroad is thus, in part, noticed by Mr. Winsor from his returns.

"The Branch-Library system of the larger libraries partially obviates the necessity of increasing duplicates in each branch. Birmingham buys up to six; Manchester puts two or three copies, at most, in each branch; Liverpool, very seldom more than one copy. Where there are no branches, as at Sheffield and Nottingham, they go up in some cases as high as six or eight copies; Blackburn, two or three; Salford, three, etc."

Again, of the replies given to that inquiry of the Circular, "What proportion of your purchases are novels?" Mr. Winsor writes thus, respecting the foreign libraries: —

"In several of these libraries, the usual proportion of novels in their increase is about one-third. At Bolton, England, it is fifty per cent.; at Birmingham, twenty per cent.; at Sheffield novels form sixteen per cent. of their library."

"Some of the associated libraries obviate the necessity of buying largely of this class of books, by paying a fixed sum to Mudie's or some other London library, which furnishes them to any extent desired with duplicates of popular books, to be withdrawn when the demand slackens."

For the year reported in Mr. Winsor's tables, in the column headed "Sale of Duplicates," the Holton Library returns the number twenty.

XIV. CATALOGUE.

It is hoped that a new Catalogue will be ready for the press in the summer. Since the issue of the first Catalogue in June, 1866, the number of books has been nearly doubled; and written supplements are furnished at the Hall. It has been contemplated to print only a supplement of books added since 1866, but the Library Committee, on a full review of the subject, have lately reported in favor of a whole Catalogue. They have come to this conclusion on various considerations, — not the least of which is the generally expressed desire of those using the Library, from all classes and sections of the town, that one complete Catalogue may be furnished them, instead of one new half to be laid with one old half already not a little worn. The expense of printing an entire Catalogue will not exceed very much the cost of a Supplement only. And after a whole Catalogue is thus procured, the titles of books purchased each year may be appended to the Trustees' Annual Report, somewhat after the plan of the Monthly Bulletins at the Boston Public Library, and so no further Catalogue be required for many years. Much dissatisfaction is manifested with the present condition of the Catalogues by all who have occasion to consult them at home, or at the Hall. Some inaccuracies occurred in the first Catalogue, prepared, as it was necessarily, in haste. A more approved system than the present of numbering the books, namely, by alcoves and shelves, could be introduced in a new Catalogue. The Trustees are not at liberty to use the legacy of the founder for printing a Catalogue. But the citizens, it is believed, will now regard a complete and well arranged Catalogue as indispensable for their convenience. The Auditors entirely concurring with the Trustees in the generally acknowledged necessity of such a work, will include in their estimate for the appropriations of the coming year a small sum for this purpose.

XV. READING ROOM.

Our Reading Room is visited on each day and evening of delivery, by more or less persons of either sex, for reading and for consultation of books. Indeed, with a good number of books, which from their cost, or size, or terms of bequest, or other considerations, cannot be loaned, but must remain "Books of Reference," such an appendage to the Library becomes quite essential. On the tables are found sixteen of the leading Periodicals, Reviews, and Magazines. Of the eighty-eight libraries in Massachusetts, replying to the Circular addressed to them from Boston, as named on page 14 of this Report, sixty-three are returned as without a Reading Room and Periodicals. The remaining twenty-five we have classed in the following table as maintaining Reading Rooms, with the number of Periodicals furnished in each.

Boston Public Library, nearly 300 Periodicals.

Boston Athenæum,	115	Brighton Holton Library,	16
Boston Natural Historical Society,	100	Boston Library of 1794,	15
		Taunton Public Library,	15
Worcester Public Library,	45	Lowell Young Men's Christian Association,	13
Boston Young Men's Christian Association,	40	Westfield Athenæum,	12
Boston Mercantile Library,	35	Waltham Public Library,	11
New Bedford Public Library,	31	Northampton Public Library,	10
Amherst College Library,	30	Boston New Church,	10
Salem Athenæum,	29	Lynn Public Library,	9
Brookline Public Library,	25	Roxbury Athenæum,	8
Lawrence Pacific Mills,	23	Stockbridge Jackson Library,	6
Andover Theolog. Seminary,	20	Gardner Young Men's Christian Association,	5
Newton Theological "	19		

Charlestown Public Library reports a Reading Room and Periodicals, but not the number.

Several of the Massachusetts Reading Rooms are likewise supplied with newspapers. We select a few libraries within the United States and British America from the voluminous returns furnished as above, and set them here in order, with the number of periodicals and newspapers supplied in their Reading Rooms.

The two smallest named are Indianapolis, Ind., State Library, four periodicals and "several" newspapers; and Newport, R. I., Public Library, five periodicals and fifteen newspapers. Some of the largest Reading Rooms, report thus: —

NAMES.	Periodicals.	Newspapers	NAMES.	Periodicals.	Newspapers.
Brooklyn, N. Y., Mercantile,	210	66	Philadelphia Mercantile,	100	200
New York Cooper Union,	204	55	New York Society Library,	100	30
New York Mercantile,	150	200	San Francisco,	80	300
Washington Lib. Cong.	132	58	St. Louis Pub. Library,	76	16

In British America, Ottawa, Library of Parliament returns one hundred and thirty Periodicals; and Quebec Literary and Historical Society returns twenty-two Periodicals, neither naming newspapers.

XV. LIBRARY BUILDING.

Each year, with its stated increase of books, makes more manifest to us the need of a separate building in which these acquisitions may be safely kept. As at present accommodated, they are not without peril from fire. We have paid for books, now in the Library, between five and six thousand dollars, as shown by the six annual Reports of the Treasurer. And in this estimate is not included two thousand volumes presented by the Brighton Library Association, and by the town, on starting. Neither is there included three hundred and seventy-five volumes, many of them of considerable cost, which have been presented by individual donors. Nine thousand dollars would be required to replace as many books as we have, with the same titles, and in the same editions. In view of the growing value of the Library, the Trustees have just taken out another policy of insurance for three thousand dollars, additional to what had been before effected. The subject of a new Library Building the Trustees have brought to the notice of their fellow-citizens in former Reports. In their last Report, particularly, edifices then in process of erection, as at Brookline and at Newton, were described from the architects' plans, and such considerations presented as might show the extreme desirableness of a new building here. On page 12, of this Report, it may be seen that a very beautiful and commodious edifice in wood was, last year, erected at Hingham, at an expense of only twelve thousand dollars, part of the munificent donation of Hon. Mr. Fearing. It might not be judicious to build in wood here, in the suburbs of the good old city, that, as intimated above, is so soon to embrace beneath her motherly wings all this outlying territory, and engraft our library, as a branch, on her noble stock. But an edifice of some kind will soon be imperatively required, if we would maintain even the present ratio of increase, and even our present relative position among similar institutions.

The town was not satisfied, in earlier days, that her school edifices should rank behind those of her neighbors. But before most of the towns in her vicinity, before several of the cities of the Commonwealth had banished all those uncouth school-houses of a former generation, she had remodelled and furnished every school edifice in her borders after the most approved modern patterns. The town has, doubtless, deferred an [appropriation for a building thus far, lest, by such action, she might anticipate the wish of some generous-hearted son to connect his own name with the edifice. We shall ever honor the name of our founder, Mr.

Holton, who, while endowing a Library for his native town, bequeathed besides between eighty and ninety thousand dollars of his ample estate to charitable purposes here and elsewhere. But we need honor him no less, while with him honoring some other who shall now generously provide a building. While the name of Holton attaches to the books he gave and gives, how gracefully should another name attach to the Hall that holds them! Indeed, these pleasant fancies have well-nigh borne us on into the consciousness that a building has been promised; and, as good sponsors, we volunteer a form, through which it may be called, leaving but a single blank to be filled with the donor's name: —

The   Hall of the Holton Library.

XVI. BOOKS ADDED LAST YEAR.

We have added, the past year, by purchase and donation, nearly nine hundred volumes, exclusive of pamphlets. Many of these pamphlets will immediately go upon the shelves as bound books. The titles of these additional volumes, not on the printed catalogues, will be found on the supplements at the Hall. They embrace a good proportion of the most desirable works in the English tongue, for a free Public Library, which the year has furnished. A small part only of the additions are works of fiction. Entire sets of the works of the standard writers of fiction are already on the shelves; and each year we keep those sets complete as new works appear. But apart from these leading works of fiction, we have found occasion to add but very few other novels. Indeed, under works of fiction, in these modern times, are embraced many of the finest productions, and most to be commended. Formerly the novel, and for the most part, all that went under the name of fiction was here included, was held the great terror of all conservators of good morals and pure taste. Certainly the records of English and French literature, to go no further back than the last century, amply justify such judgment. Nor do we deny that the low, sensational novel, ministering to the grossest passions, pandering to the vilest tastes, still creeps stealthily forth from the press, and finds victims enough for its soul-destroying work. Our doors give no entrance to such books. Their place is fitly named in the fifth verse of the fifth chapter of Proverbs, — a place, the gorgeous upholstery possibly, and gilded alcoves of which we shall not stop to picture. But to class with such pests as these all the works of modern fiction,—to put under the ban, Scott, Dickens, Curtis, Mitchell, Winthrop, Arthur, Austen, Bronté, and Evans, Whitney, Phelps, and Alcott, Child, and Stowe, Cooper, and Edgeworth, Hawthorne, Sargent, and Holmes, Marryatt, and Reid, and Reed, Thackeray, and Higginson, and Thoreau, Mühlbach, and Muloch, Southworth, and Cummins, and Warner, and Wood, — men and women in multitudes like these, who have written and are writing in fiction that inspires, uplifts, instructs, and regenerates the race, were most unwise.

Mrs. Harriet Beecher Stowe's "Uncle Tom's Cabin" is fiction; so is Mrs. Child's "Romance of the Republic." But the whole substructure of these works is stern, terrible, historical truth, and their influence in tenderest pity and in thunder tones of warning have served — how much ! — the cause of righteousness and freedom. How, indeed, shall words measure all the good which has been wrought, intellectual, moral, religious; all the help rendered to history, science, philosophy, ethics, yes, to piety, by the best writers of fiction in this century alone? But the subject was treated so particularly in the last Report of your Trustees, and statements there furnished showing the smaller proportion of novels bought and used in this Library than in many other Public Libraries at home and abroad, that nothing need be added now.

Of course, more books, numerically, could have been put into the Library, last year, than have been furnished. But with so good a stock of standard English works in almost every department of literature, our ambition, now, is to add fresh books, — such as come daily from the press; such as the people, generally, are reading and talking about. The titles of the eight or nine hundred last added show no little variety. The lighter and the graver works, volumes of lower cost, and volumes, many of four and five dollars each, are embraced.

Biography is very fully represented, from the two imposing volumes, just published, of the Life of Daniel Webster, by George T. Curtis, one of the literary executors of the great statesman, whose works in six volumes, and whose correspondence in two volumes, we already had; from the Life of Rufus Choate, by Brown, and of Jared Sparks, by Ellis; from the Life of Judge Smith, by Rev. Dr. Morison, and the Life of Rev. John Murray; from the Life of Columbus; from the Life of John Bright of England, and of Gladstone; the Life of Miss Milford, in two volumes; and of Audubon, the great Naturalist, by his widow; to the less-pretending, but deeply interesting Life of Craig, the faithful minister, and to the touching Memoir of James P. Walker, the devoted friend and laborer in the cause of Sunday schools. Included, moreover, is that work which is charming so many readers in this country and abroad, Diary, Reminiscences, and Correspondence of Henry Crabb Robinson, in two volumes; Reminiscences, also, of Hamilton; of Mendelssohn; the Life of Ida Lewis, brave heroine of Lime Rock; Memoirs of Keble, in two volumes, by Coleridge; the new edition of Keble's Poems, being likewise entered in its own department; Abbott's Joseph Napoleon, and even Pollard's Life of Jefferson Davis.

Among works of travels, we see the titles of the great work of Raphael Pumpelly, Professor in Harvard University, Across America and Asia, a Five-years' Journey around the World; Our New West, by Bowles; Italy, Florence, Venice, by Taine; Down the Rhine, by William T. Adams; Life in Australia, by Boot, one of the five-dollar volumes; Notes in

England and Italy, by Mrs. Hawthorne; Our New Way Round the World, by Carleton; Twelve Nights in a Hunter's Camp; Eight Years in England, by Baker; Abyssinia Described, fully and beautifully; Fellows's Travels and Researches in Asia Minor, finely illustrated, as are many of the books we name; Deserts of North America, by Domeneck, in two volumes, of the price of six dollars; An American Family in Paris; Yo Semite Guide, by Josiah Dwight Whitney, Professor in Harvard University, another of the most costly volumes; Baker's Tributaries of the Nile; Wanderings in China, by Fortune; Letters from the East, and Letters of a Traveller, both by our poet, Bryant; and Adams's new work on Pompeii.

In History we have added last year, to name only a few among many works, Prehistoric Nations; Hellas, by Chase; A Treatise on the Salem Withcraft; Town Records of Salem, from 1634 to 1649; Drake's valuable work on The Annals of Witchcraft,— these all additional to Upham's large work on the Salem Witchcraft, which was in the Library before; Early History of Vermont; Spain and the Spanish, in two volumes, by Mrs. Byrne; Reminiscences of Amherst College, by Hitchcock; History of Pittsfield, by Smith; of Essex, by Crowell; of Winchendon, by Marvin; Lossing's Field Book, of the War of 1812, in addition to all of his previous works; these few latter works being among the largest and costliest; History of the Waldenses, in two volumes; Bowles's Colorado; Sherwood's Comic History of the United States; Discovery of the West, by Francis Parkman, additional to the four other admirable works on kindred topics by this most gifted young author, and to his Treatise on the Rose, all which we had before. And still on, we see the titles of Hittell's Resources of California; Great Hunting Grounds of the World; first volume of the History of Rome, by Mommsen; Lord's Ancient States and Empires; Hagenback's History of the Church in the Eighteenth and Nineteenth Centuries; MacLean's Apostles of Mediæval Europe; and Professor

Hedge's Primeval World of Hebrew Tradition, which has attracted so widely the attention of thoughtful readers.

In Natural History, we have added, with other works, the recent large work of Wood,—Bible Animals. For the sum of four or five dollars is furnished this ample volume, in which all "beasts of the field, fowls of the air, and fishes of the sea," named in the Bible, are described and illustrated. Intelligence of Animals, by Menault, and Insect Architecture, by Rennie, most interesting, awaken the old question of difference between Reason and Instinct. The fifth great Treatise of Figuier on Reptiles and Birds has been added, at a cost of five dollars; copiously and beautifully illustrated as are his four other elaborate treatises, before in the Library: The Insect World, The World before the Deluge, The Vegetable World, and The Ocean World.

In Geology, Denton's Lectures, or Our Planet, is added. In Political Economy, Greeley's Treatise; and the History of Socialism, by John H. Noyes; and Laws of Business, by Theophilus Parsons. In Physiology, Flint's third volume, or part, of which we had parts first and second, also Phillips' large and able work, of interest to all, Treatment of the Eye. In Natural Science, the year has furnished Lackland's Treatise on Meteors; Wonders of the Deep; The Polar World, by Dr. G. Hartwig; Treatises, severally, on Wonders of Heat, on Volcanoes and Earthquakes; on Wonders of Optics; on Thunder and Lightning; and, larger than these, and at a cost of five or six dollars, Mysteries of the Ocean.

In Horticulture, we have added Flagg's work on European Vineyards; Pear Culture for Profit, by Quinn; Downing's Fruits and Fruit Trees of America, at a cost of six dollars; Among the Trees, by Mary J. Losimer; Planting the Wilderness, by Pearson; Trees, Plants and Flowers, and How They Grow.

Yet further among recent titles, we read Mülbachh's Goethe and Schiller; The Age of Elizabeth, by our first American Essayist, Edwin P. Whipple, additional to all his previous works, which the Library already contained; J. S. C. Abbott's Romance of Spanish History; The Ingham Papers, by Rev. Edward Everett Hale; our poet, Lowell's Cathedral, and Tennyson's Holy Grail and Other Poems, making complete in the Library the published works of these four writers. In like manner have been added Auerbach's Villa on the Rhine; Life, Speeches, and Discourses of Père Hyacinthe; Woman, her Rights, Wrongs, Privileges, and Responsibilities, by Prockett; Bushnell's Woman's Suffrage; Mrs. Whitney's Hitherto; Mrs. Stowe's, Mrs. Dall's, Miss Alcott's, and Miss Phelps's works, of the past year; Man and Woman, Equal but Unlike, by James Reed; The London Illustrated News, in sixteen volumes, folio, most fully illustrated; Nat, the Navigator, presenting our noble Bowditch as an example for boys; Carpenters' and Builders' Guide, by Plumer; Practical Poultry Keeper, by Wright; a highly approved Treatise on Dreams, Sleep, and its Phenomena, Wakefulness, and Somnambulism, by Dr. Hammond, Professor in the Bellevue Hospital of New York; Men and Things at Washington; History of American Manufactures, in three volumes, by Bishop, with several hundred steel-plate portraits of the leading manufacturers of the country, in various departments,—a work costing nine dollars; Night Scenes in the Bible, an elegantly illustrated volume; and a second volume, Metrical Pieces, of which we had the first, by Rev. Dr. Frothingham of Boston; this latter, collected before he reached his present infirmity of age, but telling, like all his various productions, of rare intellectual gifts which, in the years past, have placed him foremost among American scholars and divines.

But in thus naming, for the convenience of our readers until a new catalogue is furnished, single works from among a multitude of books added last year, we are possibly enacting the old folly of the man who carried about a single brick to show the house he would dispose of. Leaving all, we hasten to close. And be it with the hope that each book, both those just added and those before in store, if not a well-formed and comely brick, may be as "polished cornerstones," of which the Bible tells, in that fair "palace" of knowledge which all good readers build. Various, of course, are the merits of the books selected. The above titles, as indicating classes of books, tell something of their character. Some perhaps may lull; some, we are sure, must stir and task and keep awake all the energies of mind and heart. Jean Paul, who said many good things, uttered no truer saying than this: "There are a few powerful authors who punish their readers, as did the Roman tyrants of old, by depriving them of sleep; but most writers are too benevolent to do this." May the books presented here, if of the former class, rouse and incite to right living and noble action. If of the latter class, may they at least induce a healthful rest from the strife of passion, from the cares and perplexities of the world; the sleep, at least, may it be of pleasant dreams.

Respectfully submitted, in behalf of the Trustees,
FREDERIC A. WHITNEY,
President.

FREDERIC A. WHITNEY,
WEARE DOW BICKFORD,
WEBSTER FRANKLIN WARREN, *Librarian,*
DAVID TURNER PACKARD.

WILLIAM WIRT WARREN,
CHARLES HENRY BASS BRECK,
GRANVILLE FULLER,
JOHN PERKINS CUSHING WINSHIP.

EDMUND RICE,
LIFE BALDWIN, *Treasurer,*
WILLIAM FREDERIC MATCHETT,
BELA STODDARD FISKE, *Secretary.*

Trustees by triennial, biennial, and annual election.

HOLTON LIBRARY, January 31, 1870.

REPORT

OF THE

LIBRARIAN OF THE HOLTON LIBRARY.

To the Trustees:

The Librarian herewith submits the sixth Annual Report for the year ending January 31, 1870.

The Library is at present in the following condition: —

Number of volumes belonging to the Library at the commencement of the year,	5,008
Number of volumes added by purchase, and by binding periodicals,	781
Number of volumes presented,	56
	5,845
Number of volumes purchased to supply places of books worn out, defaced, or lost,	7
Total number of volumes February 1, 1870,	5,838
Number of pamphlets February 1, 1869,	1,185
" added by presentation,	116
" purchase,	376
Total number of pamphlets added to February 1, 1870,	1,677
No. of subscribers, or card-holders, Feb. 1, 1869,	1,559
" " added the past year,	186
Total " " since the opening of the Library in 1864,	1,745

Number of subscribers who have taken out books during the past year, ... 881
Number of books taken out during the year, . . 15,377
Average number to each subscriber, . . . 17+
Number of days (including evenings) on which the Library has been open, ... 94
Average number taken out each day, . . . 164
Amount expended for books, periodicals, and stationery, ... $1,174 91
Amount received from fines, ... $56 17

PERIODICALS.

Atlantic Monthly.	Harper's Weekly.
Cornhill Magazine.	Leslie's Magazine.
Eclectic Magazine.	Littell's Living Age.
Every Saturday.	North American Review.
Galaxy.	Our Young Folks' Magazine.
Genealogical Register.	Punch.
Godey's Magazine.	Scientific American.
Harper's Magazine.	The Horticulturist.

The foregoing Report embraces the year ending January 31, 1870, excepting as regards the lost books. As the intermission is now taken during the month of August, instead of February, as was formerly the practice, and the examination of the Library made in August, the statement concerning books lost relates to the year ending July 31, 1869. Eight books appear to have been lost during the year, to wit: "Sketches of Irish Character," "Manners and Customs of Principal Nations," "Planchette," "Services at the Death of Abraham Lincoln," "Rob Roy, Vol. I.," "Dog Crusoe," "Edmond Daults," and "Volume Thirty of Harper's Monthly Magazine."

The titles of the lost books are published, upon the supposition that some of them may yet be among the citizens of the town, and with the hope that all who may at any time have had either of the books in their possession, will ascertain whether they have ever returned them to the Library.

Appended is a list of the donors for the past year, with the number of volumes and pamphlets presented by each.

All of which is respectfully submitted,

W. F. WARREN, *Librarian.*

HOLTON LIBRARY, Jan. 31, 1870.

BENEFACTORS

TO THE

HOLTON LIBRARY,

FOR THE YEAR 1869-70.

And the Number of Volumes and Pamphlets received from each.

JAMES HOLTON'S ORIGINAL BEQUEST, $6,000.

Names and Residence.	Pamphlets.	Volumes.
Baldwin, Life, Brighton	20	1
Bates, Joseph L., Boston	2	3
Boston Public Library, Trustees of	7	–
Boston School for the Ministry, Officers of	1	–
Boutwell, George S. Hon., Washington, D. C.	9	9
Bradlee, Caleb Davis, Rev., Boston	–	9
Brighton, Town of	–	1
Capen, Barnard, Boston	–	12
Dana, Esther, Mrs., Brighton	–	1
Greenleaf, Richard Cranch, Boston	25	3
Hooper, Dwight B., Mrs., Brighton	–	7
Kirke, George W., Brighton	–	2
Manchester Public Library, Trustees of	1	–
Massachusetts, Commonwealth of	–	5
Matchett, William F., Brighton	16	–
Packard, David T., Rev., "	3	

Peabody Institute, Trustees of, Peabody .	1	
Reading Public Library, Trustees of, .	1	
Sibley, John L., Cambridge . . .	2	
Taunton Public Library, Trustees of .	1	
Turner, Alfred T., Boston . . .	1	
Watertown Public Library, Trustees of .	1	–
Whitney, Frederic A., Mrs., Brighton .	–	2
Whitney, Frederic A., Rev., " . .	–	1
Winship, J. P. C., " . .	23	–
Winsor, Justin, Boston	1	–
Worcester Public Library, Directors of, .	1	–
	116	56

TREASURER'S REPORT.

Life Baldwin, Treasurer, in account with Holton Library.

Dr.

To balance of funds on hand, as per last report, Feb. 6, 1869,		$4,388 19
To sale of coupons,	$114 00	
Premium on do.,	42 18	
		156 18
To cash received of Librarian for		
Fines 3 months, ending May 1,	$10 56	
" 3 " " Aug. 1,	18 30	
" 3 " " Nov. 1,	11 04	
" 3 " " Feb. 1,	16 27	
		56 17
To sale of coupons,	$111 00	
Premium on do.,	22 75	
		133 75
To Premium on $400 U. S. bonds sold,		57 11
		$4,791 40

Cr.

By cash paid sundry bills and expenses, as follows, viz. : —

By Rice & Rogers, printing, etc.,	$11 25
W. F. Warren, sundry bills,	45 35
Nichols & Noyes, books,	1,035 31
Check stamps,	60

M. H. Sargent, Jr., books,		3 00
E. E. Rice & Co., labels,		2 75
Hooper, Lewis & Co., paper,		8 00
Bela S. Fiske, insurance,		121 00
H. Cushman, expressage,		9 70
Crosby & Daniels, books,		68 00
Lovering & Co., books,		1 25
Balance on hand in U. S. Bonds,	$3,400 00	
Cash,	85 19	
		3,485 19
		$4,791 40

L. BALDWIN, *Treasurer.*

BRIGHTON, Feb. 8, 1870.

SEVENTH AND EIGHTH ANNUAL REPORTS

OF THE

TRUSTEES

OF THE

HOLTON LIBRARY,

BRIGHTON.

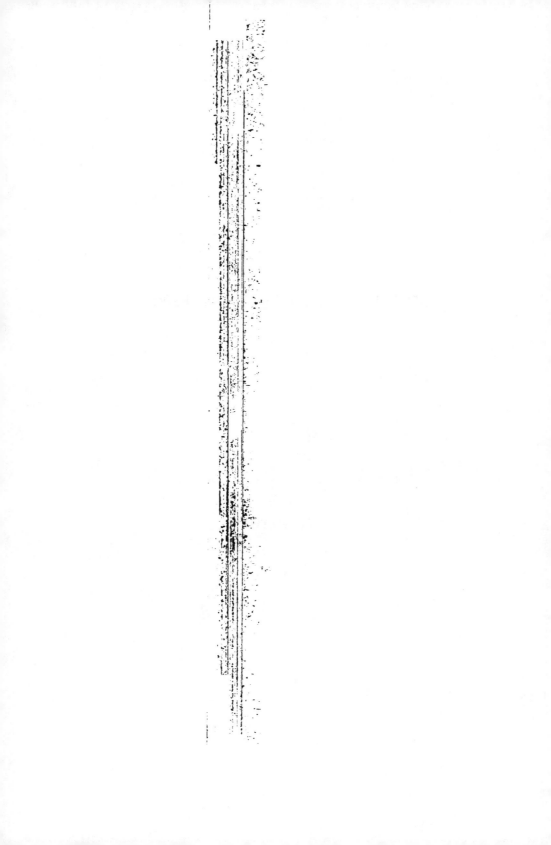

SEVENTH AND EIGHTH ANNUAL REPORTS

OF THE

TRUSTEES

OF THE

HOLTON LIBRARY,

BRIGHTON,

FOR 1870-71, AND 1871-72.

BOSTON:
ALFRED MUDGE & SON, PRINTERS, 34 SCHOOL STREET.
1872.

TOWN OF BRIGHTON.

HOLTON LIBRARY,* April 1, 1872.

TO THE AUDITORS:

Gentlemen, — I have the honor to transmit to you, herewith, the seventh and eighth annual reports of the Trustees of the Holton Library, prepared in obedience to the ordinance adopted by the town April 8, 1864.

Yours respectfully,

W. F. WARREN,
Secretary of the Board of Trustees.

---

* The preparation of this document was unavoidably delayed beyond the regular date of February 1.

TRUSTEES

Of the Library from its commencement.

	Elected.	Ret'd.
BALDWIN, HENRY	1872	
BALDWIN, LIFE	1864	
BENNETT, JOSEPH	1870	
BENYON, ABNER INGALLS	1866—1868	
BICKFORD, WEARE DOW	1864—1872	
BRECK, CHARLES HENRY BASS	1867—	
CUSHMAN, JOHN PAINE	1864—1866	
FISKE, BELA STODDARD	1865—1870	
" " "	1872	
FULLER, GRANVILLE	1864	
HUTCHINSON, CHARLES CARROLL	1864—1865	
JACKSON, NATHANIEL	1864—1869	
MATCHETT, THEODORE	1864—1867	
MATCHETT, WILLIAM FREDERIC	1867—1872	
PACKARD, DAVID TEMPLE	1869	
*POND, JOSEPH ADAMS	1864—1867	
RICE, EDMUND	1865	
RUGGLES, JOHN	1864—1865	
WARREN, WEBSTER FRANKLIN	1869	
WARREN, WILLIAM WIRT	1864	
WHITNEY, FREDERIC AUGUSTUS	1864	
WINSHIP, JOHN PERKINS CUSHING	1864	

* Deceased, October 28, 1867.

OFFICERS

Of the Library from its commencement.

PRESIDENTS.

	Elected.	Retired.
JOHN RUGGLES,	April 18, 1864 — October 9, 1865.	
FREDERIC AUGUSTUS WHITNEY,	November 13, 1865 —	

SECRETARIES.

JOHN PERKINS CUSHING WINSHIP,	April 18, 1864 — March 13, 1865.
BELA STODDARD FISKE,	March 13, 1865 — March 14, 1870.
WEBSTER FRANKLIN WARREN,	March 14, 1870 —

TREASURER.

LIFE BALDWIN,   May 23, 1864 —

LIBRARIANS.

JOHN PERKINS CUSHING WINSHIP,	June 13, 1864 — July 9, 1866.
WEBSTER FRANKLIN WARREN,	July 9, 1866 —

PRESENT LIBRARY SERVICE.

WEBSTER FRANKLIN WARREN, *Librarian.*
HERBERT LANGDON WATERMAN, *First Assistant.*
EDWIN OSGOOD KIMBALL, *Second Assistant.*
Miss MARY JANE BOWKER, *Third Assistant.*

THE special attention of parents and guardians of the young is called to the following law of the Commonwealth : —

"Whoever wilfully and wantonly writes upon, injures, defaces, tears, or destroys any book, plate, picture, engraving, or statue belonging to any law, town, city, or other public library, shall be punished by a fine of not less than five dollars, nor more than one thousand dollars, for every such offence."

SEVENTH AND EIGHTH ANNUAL REPORTS

OF THE

TRUSTEES OF THE HOLTON LIBRARY.

IN obedience to the Ordinance respecting the Holton Library, adopted by the Town of Brighton April 8, 1864, the Trustees have the honor to submit their seventh and eighth Annual Reports as one joint

REPORT.

Last year, as may be remembered, at the stated time for issuing the Trustees' Report, the Library was undergoing a thorough revision, and was closed. No books were given out for many months. The Trustees made no report. The last report issued was the sixth, extending to February 1, 1870. The period at present to be reported on begins accordingly with that date. And that the regular file of reports may not be interrupted, this document is denominated the seventh and eighth reports.

LIBRARY ENLARGED.

From over this interval of months, the Trustees have first to congratulate the citizens on a greatly enlarged library. Several hundred pamphlets, some of rare value and interest, have been prepared for use, partly bound, arranged in pamphlet-cases, and numbered in the catalogue where they can be selected, and may be consulted and read at the hall as books. Including these, the entire collection now comprises something over nine thousand volumes. From the statistics of ,public libraries in Massachusetts, gathered a few years since, it appears that this Library is equalled in numbers by only two or three of the town libraries. The several city libraries of the State have larger collections.

ARRANGEMENT OF BOOKS.

Then the arrangement of the books is far better than before. Hitherto, the books were placed side by side in the order in which they came to the Library. Number 4,325, for example, when purchased, must stand next to 4,324, though, perhaps, the former volume was a poem, and the latter a treatise on the mathematics. Now, on a wiser plan, which may be found explained in the preface to the new catalogue, books are placed together according to subjects, and so numbered on the shelves of each alcove.

SECOND, OR NEW CATALOGUE.

In the last report of the Trustees, mention was made of the new Catalogue, for which a special appropriation was to be asked at the approaching town meeting, and which was expected to be prepared in the ensuing summer.

It was begun at that season named. But the magnitude of the work was not justly apprehended; and as by the new method adopted, the whole order of the library was necessarily changed, much more time than had been expected was required for the completion of the catalogue. The work has been finely printed by Messrs. Alfred Mudge & Son, of Boston, in an octavo volume of 354 pages; an edition of 1,500 copies for $1,650. It comprises, besides its own preface, the preface of the first Holton Library Catalogue of 1866, containing some interesting historical facts. It comprises, also, the rules and regulations; the names of past and present Trustees and officers; a large dictionary of Pseudonyms, or assumed names of authors, most of which occur in the catalogue, and which will be of as much value to other libraries as to our own; a complete list of donors to the Library, with their donations, and likewise Bulletin No. I. The catalogue is prepared with special reference to the indefinite increase of the library in the contemplated new edifice, where the alcoves, at present numbering eighteen, will be multiplied above the ground floor in galleries, and will be both wider and deeper. The Trustees of the Boston City Library, through their courteous and efficient Superintendent and Secretary, Mr. Justin Winsor, have furnished us complete sets of their publications, — Catalogues, Supplements, Bulletins, and various documents, — which are properly arranged in the catalogue, with reference to the approaching annexation of Brighton with Boston, when our Library becomes, of course, a branch of the Boston City Library.

BULLETINS.

It is contemplated to issue successive Bulletins as they may be demanded by the accumulation of books, and thus another complete catalogue, which involves necessarily a considerable expense, will not be required for many years. Book-titles in the catalogue, referred to the Bulletin, and not found in Bulletin No. I, appended to the catalogue, may be understood as in preparation for a subsequent Bulletin.

SERVICE ON THE CATALOGUE.

The work of compiling and superintending the catalogue has devolved on the President of the Board, who desires here to acknowledge the aid of the librarian, Mr. Warren, and of his two assistants, Herbert Langdon, son of the late Joseph Langdon Waterman, and Edwin Osgood, son of J. K. Kimball, both of this town. He has also been aided by several young ladies, — particularly by Miss Clara Adelia, daughter of George Washington Wentworth, and Miss Mary Jane, daughter of Thomas Washington Bowker, both of this town, who have been very faithfully and patiently employed to the completion of the work, and who have gained much valuable information respecting authors and their works, the labor of cataloguing, and the Library in general. The wearisome details of such a labor in all the *minutiæ* of alphabetical arrangement, of foreign idioms in names and titles, of classification, of size of volumes, of their place and date of publication, of book-numbers and labels, of alcoves and shelves, can be known only through experience. Other young ladies who have assisted for shorter periods since the work was begun, are Miss Clara Stone Stevens, of Farmington, Me.; Miss Sarah Dana, daughter of Daniel Osborn, Miss Fannie Warren, daughter of Charles Currier, together with Mr. Thomas P. Bray, all of this town.

TREASURER'S REPORTS.

The last two reports of the treasurer, Mr. Life Baldwin, covering the years 1870–71 and 1871–72, are appended. He has served faithfully in this office since the establishment of the Library. From them will be learned the condition of the invested fund, and the expenses, so far as they are defrayed from the treasury of the Holton Library. The town, it will be remembered, each year, supplements the income of the invested fund with a special appropriation. The additional appropriation for the ensuing year is one thousand five hundred dollars.

LIBRARIAN'S REPORT.

The report of the librarian, Mr Warren, to be found, also, with the accompanying documents, is understood, likewise, to cover the last two years. As the Library was closed for a considerable period during the revision and the preparation of the catalogue, his statements and figures are of course very imperfect as annual tabular records. The old interest, however, was soon manifested on the reopening of the Library to the public. The improved method of keeping the Library accounts, of the delivery and return of books, and the new form of cards introduced, have met with very great favor.

THE READING-ROOM.

All card-holders have the privileges of the reading-room. The tables are furnished with the leading reviews and periodicals. Conversation is forbidden here by the established rules and regulations, to which all have signed compliance on taking their cards. All have the opportunity to read here undisturbed through the whole time, day or evening, during which the Library is open. One may likewise consult and read here, not only the reviews, magazines, etc., but also pamphlets which have been arranged in the pamphlet-cases, and any book contained on the catalogues by requesting the loan of it of the librarian, or of the assistant in attendance, and returning the same to him again before leaving the hall.

DONATIONS.

More books and pamphlets have been presented to the Library since the last report was issued than during any other similar period since its establishment. They have come from all quarters, and from names among the most eminent of the land. Our senator in Congress, Hon. Charles Sumner, and our representative in Congress, Hon. George Merrill Brooks; our late senator in the Massachusetts legislature, Hon. William Wirt Warren, and our late representative in the legislature, Hon. George Henry Howe, both of this town, have, with the Secretary of the Commonwealth, kept complete our valuable files of national, State, and other documents, while all of them, likewise, have made other contributions.

The names of Hon. Charles Francis Adams, of Henry Whitney Bellows, D. D., of New York, of Hon. Josiah Quincy, of Hon. James Brooks of the United States Senate, are among recent donors. The elegant clock, for which it was stated, in the last published report of the Trustees, funds had been given by Mrs. William Frederic Matchett, of this town (three hundred dollars), but which had not then arrived, was set up in its place in the inner hall, May 6, 1870. The American Peace Society, the Society for the Prevention of Cruelty to Animals, the American Tract Society, have made contributions. The Massachusetts Bible Society has given us both the English Bible and the English Testament in large and handsome editions; and in neat, though smaller editions, Bibles and Testaments, separate, in the French and German languages. The American Unitarian Association has presented interesting and valuable books, all in new copies, of the estimated value of more than fifty dollars. The President, Mr. Eliot, and several professors of Harvard University, have been donors. The Boston City Library, through its President, Mr. William Whitwell Greenough, and its Superintendent, Mr. Justin Winsor, has kept us as completely supplied with all her publications as if annexation were already accomplished, and ours was, indeed, a branch-library of that grand maternal stock. To the Trustees of the public libraries of Brookline, Charlestown, Hingham, Manchester, N. H., of the Meadville Theological School, Pennsylvania, of the public libraries of Milton, Newton, of the Peabody Institute, Danvers, and of the Peabody Institute, Peabody, of Quincy, of Reading, of the Redwood Library and Athenæum in Newport, R. I., of the Silas Bronson Library in Waterbury, Conn., of Taunton, of Waltham, of Watertown, of Worcester, we are indebted for these two years past, now reported, for catalogues, reports, and other books and pamphlets.

Our constant and generous donor, the Rev. Caleb Davis Bradlee, of Boston, has in these last two years sent works in handsome bindings, of which the smallest estimated value on our books exceeds one hundred and fifty dollars. The single volume of largest cost, received from any donor (sixteen dollars), has come from a frequent contributor, an esteemed lady of Boston, recently deceased, Mrs. John S. Tyler, whose father, Mr. Abiel Winship, was born in this place, and whose grandfather, Mr. Jonathan Winship, Sen., was most intimately identified as an influential citizen with the town. The volume referred to, which was accompanied by several others from Mrs. Tyler, shortly before her death, is a large quarto, superbly illustrated, " Pages and Pictures, from the writings of James Fennimore Cooper, by his daughter, Susan F. Cooper."

Hon. Albert Fearing, Hon. Isaac Livermore, Mr. Samuel G. Drake, Mr. Frederic Kidder, Mr. John H. Sheppard, Mr. Edmund B. Whitney, and Mr. Henry Austin Whitney, all of Boston, have made us valuable donations. Mr. Richard Cranch Greenleaf, of Boston, has added to his earlier and numerous benefactions, contributions, likewise, in these two years past. Mr. Joseph Loud Bates, of Boston, Secretary of the Massachusetts Charitable Mechanic Association, has added to his previous donations, so that our library has now one of the most complete collections extant of the publications of that ancient and most honorable association. From the Merchants' Insurance Company, Boston, and from its Secretary, Mr. James C. Braman, have come sixty-three volumes with pamphlets. Rev. Ezra S. Gannett, D. D., Samuel K. Lothrop, D. D., Chandler Robbins, D. D., George W. Blagden, D. D., Rev. Nathaniel Hall, all of Boston, have presented us with extensive collections of their publications. Dr. Blagden, it may be remembered, began his ministry in this town, in 1827, as first pastor of the Second Church here. Similar collections we have likewise received from Hon. John G. Palfrey, D. D., William Newell, D. D., Andrew P. Peabody, D. D., Rev. Oliver C. Everett, Rev. Prof. Edward J. Young, and Rev. Alexander McKenzie, all of Cambridge. Hon. Joseph Breck, Rev. Thomas W. Silloway, and Augustus Mason, M. D., all of this town, and Alfred Hosmer, M. D., of Watertown, have laid us under obligations for renewed favors.

We could have wished that while so many persons in other towns and cities have thus sent contributions to our alcoves, the names of more of our own citizens might have been inscribed as donors. It would seem to be matter of just pride for every citizen to do his part, — to contribute but his mite, — to send in, each year, though but a single volume or pamphlet, to help build up here a great library that shall diffuse its blessings through the community before the eyes of its patrons, and still ripen its harvests in the generations advancing. Why might not the names of one thousand among the men, women, and children of our town have been added to our donation-book the last year? Costly books need not necessarily be given, — nor rare, nor wonderful books. But a volume that its owner has read and enjoyed and been profited by, let him " cast " it on these " waters," where it may be " bread " to other minds, and so, as God's Word is true, " he shall find it " again as a benediction in the community, " after many days." " Stand not " too much " upon the order of " our giving, let Shakspeare teach us; " but " give " at once." Be not too curious to ask if this book or that will interest others; if this book is really worth giving; if really the Library will care to receive it. One's own tastes, his likes or dislikes are very fallible criteria in judging of the literary needs of all other readers. Very various must be the material gathered in our large libraries that the wants and tastes of all may be met. Can one in a hundred who frequent our public libraries in Boston and its suburbs, be called strictly literary and critical readers? As in Dante's immortal poem, various circles must be passed through before the inmost centre of critical taste and faultless literary appreciation is reached or relished. Almost any book, not objectionable on moral grounds, may find a place, and sooner or later a call, in these institutions. Do not suppose that only new books are desired. Ofttimes is found in the old books the mellow flavor, as of wine, which the new lack. High authority has said, "No man having drunk old wine straightway desireth new, because he saith the old is better." Well, Homer, Shakspeare, Milton, do not yet pale much before modern bards; nor many of the early classics in divers tongues, before more recent rhetoric. A volume has been presented to our library the past year by an esteemed lady of this town, Mrs. Margaret A. Hagar, which was printed in London in 1636. Now we would not advise every card-holder to select this very book to-morrow, as the most profitable and engaging reading for them all. But let not even Young America imagine that because " such an awful old book," it is therefore to be condemned. Its embodied thought would weigh down scores of books perhaps that date from yesterday. Yet we learned recently of one library in our country which, seeming likely to outgrow the rather limited shelf-room allotted, was, on the recommendation of one of its sagacions guardians, if the others assented, to be curtailed in its too-rapidly increasing proportions, by the rejection of each book comprised in it that was printed before the year 1810.

No! let the old books and the new books go in freely together, one as the complement of the other, each as making the other more valuable. And if to donors another suggestion may be pardoned, give not always or only what wholly approves itself to your own opinions, tastes, prejudices, but sometimes, as opportunity offers, what opposes them. Here is some proof of the size of a man's soul, that he is willing to throw into the great contest between truth and error, what makes against, as well as what confirms his own opinions. Few of all the inhabitants of the town are Spiritualists; but works of the best writers on Spiritualism have, from the beginning, gone upon our shelves. Very few of our inhabitants are Methodists or Episcopalians; but you find, and shall find more and more on our catalogues, names of trusted and revered writers in both those Christian sects. Of books from the Roman Catholic denomination, of course, a numerous body here, as in all the immediate suburbs of the city, we have not many; though in this regard we have been indebted to the kindness of that estimable Catholic priest, for some years in pastoral charge here, Rev. J. M. Finotti. His name, which we know is a benediction to many, stands prominent among our donors. We want more of the best practical Catholic books, and such, especially, as that religious denomination would be glad to have their young people read. And so in all the departments of letters, of religion and morals, of politics, of philosophy, science and art, how wide the field, how unceasing the call for contributions both from ancient time and modern, to these beneficent institutions!

PRIVATE GENEROSITY.

Our funds, our special town appropriations shall do their part; but private generosity must help. Far better for public libraries that willing hands thus aid their increase. Deeper shall the libraries be thus planted in the people's heart. Recall the munificent private gifts to the Boston Public Library: from Joshua Bates, fifty thousand dollars in gold; from John P. Bigelow, one thousand dollars; from the Franklin Club, the same; from Abbott Lawrence, ten thousand dollars; from Jonathan Phillips, thirty thousand dollars; from Mary P. Townsend, four thousand dollars. The able report of the Superintendent, Mr. Winsor, records the donations for the year ending April 30, 1871, as 9,750 volumes and 10,805 pamphlets. The greater part of all the donors made contributions each of but one or two volumes or pamphlets. So sprang into full strength, in early times, New England's best institutions. They grew out of voluntary, warm-hearted contributions, smaller or larger. They grew oftenest (shame on us in our less willing abundance) out of the penury and hard straights, out of the tears and prayers of noble, though needy men and women. The humble pecks of corn contributed from time to time by the bravesouled yeomanry of New England to their only college, that at Cambridge, "to the end that learning might not be buried in the graves of their fathers," nursed the infant institution, as world-renowned endowments, with no sacrifice, might not have done.

And so, citizens, will your Library be to you more precious, a tenfold blessing, if you have voluntarily contributed to its growth.

LIBRARY DONATIONS ELSEWHERE.

In previous reports, the Trustees have sought to keep their fellow-citizens informed of what has been done in other places through generous contributions in aid of public libraries. The last two or three reports, especially, present the particulars of some of the most munificent donations of modern times in this good cause. The ample gifts of money, as in Waterbury, Connecticut, of two hundred thousand dollars from Silas Bronson; in Newton, of fifteen thousand dollars from J. Wiley Edmands, and of other sums from individuals there; in Watertown, of one thousand dollars from Alvin Adams, of six hundred dollars from J. A. Locke, and of five hundred dollars each from H. H. Hunnewell, and from the heirs of Abijah White; in Lynn, of ten thousand dollars from Sidney B. Pratt; in Peabody and in Danvers, of the princely endowments of George Peabody; in Ipswich, of fifty thousand dollars from Augustus Heard; in Hingham, of twenty thousand dollars from Albert Fearing; in New York city, of three hundred thousand dollars from James Lenox, and in the words of his bequest, " of any further sums that shall be needed to make this the finest public library in the country," — have, in the above named reports, been detailed.

A few recent instances of similar liberality, all falling within the period over which the present report extends, may be added.

Mr. Samuel E. Sawyer, of Gloucester, has presented ten thousand dollars to the public library there, and this in addition to several other gifts previously made by him to the town. The late William Sanford Rogers, of Boston, bequeathed four thousand dollars to the Redwood Library and Athenæum at Newport, R. I. Alexander Duncan, of Providence, R. I., "decided to celebrate the last 4th of July by a subscription of ten thousand dollars for Mrs. Duncan and himself to the Providence Free Library." William Cullen Bryant, our American poet, has given to his native town, Cummington, in this State, twelve thousand five hundred dollars for a public library. William Monroe, of Concord, Mass., is erecting there a fine brick building, at a cost of fifty thousand dollars, which he presents to the town for its public library. Fifty thousand dollars have been recently donated to the town of Randolph by the widow and four surviving children of the late Col. Royal Turner. This is for founding a public library and erecting a fire-proof building. Hon. T. M. Allyn, of Hartford, Conn., has given to the Young Men's

Institute of that city, forty thousand dollars to establish a free public library and art gallery, and a clear title to a valuable building in addition. And finally, and nearer home to us, Mr. John L. Gardner, of Boston and Brookline, has generously contributed ten thousand dollars in aid of the funds of the Brookline public library. The noble gift has been fittingly acknowledged by the trustees in a handsome letter, which has readily found a place in the public prints.

ACCESSIONS OF BOOKS.

The recent accessions to our Library have placed it among the first of similar institutions in our country. The limits of the present report will not allow us to refer, as we have sometimes done, even by classes, to the various books which have been added since the last previous report. It is hoped that the patrons of the Library will find here, not only all such standard works as by right pertain to the public Library, but, likewise, such desirable works in the various departments of literature, as are issuing daily from the press; such as the people, generally, are reading; such as the age calls for; such, in short, as are required for the broad and generous culture which our times demand. The Trustees renew the request that the titles of books desired, and not found on our catalogues, be entered, together with the seeker's name, on the record kept for the purpose at the librarian's desk.

NEW LIBRARY EDIFICE.

And now, more and more sorely, presses the question, Where shall these treasures, so rapidly increasing, be conveniently and safely accommodated? They have outgrown their present depository. The halls now occupied, though more than ample for many a smaller public library, have become wholly inadequate for ours. The subject of a new and commodious edifice has long engaged the attention of the Trustees, who are unanimous in their judgment of its necessity; and who are happy to report that in this they are seconded by their fellow-citizens generally. They deem it best to put on record in this report the measures which have already been adopted; such steps as the town in its corporate action, and committees appointed by the town, have thus far taken.

The subject appears to have come before the town for the first time at the annual March meeting (14th day), 1870. Article 14th of the warrant was in these words: "To see if the town will take any action in relation to the purchase of a lot of land, and the erection of a suitable building thereon for the Public Library, and make the necessary appropriation therefor."

It was voted to refer the subject-matter of this article to a committee of three, with instructions to report at the April meeting ensuing. The moderator appointed Rev. Frederic A. Whitney, Mr. Life Baldwin, and Mr. J. P. Cushing Winship. Mr. Winship declining to serve, on account of engagements, Hon. William Wirt Warren was appointed in his place.

At the April town meeting ensuing (25th inst.), the chairman of the committee submitted and read in the Town Hall the following

REPORT.

The committee to whom, at the annual town meeting, March 14th, last, was referred the subject-matter of Article Fourteen in the warrant calling said meeting, with instructions to report thereon at the April meeting ensuing, which article was in these words: "To see if the town will take any action in relation to the purchase of a lot of land, and the erection of a suitable building thereon for the Public Library, and make the necessary appropriation therefor," respectfully report:—

That, in their judgment, it is very desirable that a suitable edifice should be erected for the town Library. The last two annual reports of the Trustees have set forth the urgent need of such a building, alike for the accommodation of the books, now rapidly increasing, and for their greater protection from the peril of fire. The present halls occupied by the Library will soon be insufficient for shelf-room, and they afford now no extra apartments for storage and for the preparation of books, — covering, labelling, cataloguing, and repairing, which are deemed essential to a public library. These same halls, it may be observed, may be converted into offices, and made perhaps a source of income to the town, sufficient to defray in part the interest on the appropriation for a new library edifice. Your committee do not think it necessary to enlarge upon the value and importance of a well-provided public library to a town. Nearly six years have passed since, by the generosity of one of our native-born citizens, Mr. James Holton, our Library was established and opened. It has secured the interest and the favor of all classes of our citizens. The privileges of its books loaned and the privileges of its reading-room are very generally and gladly shared. It has been the aim of the Trustees to place on its shelves, besides the standard works, all the most desirable books in American and English literature, as they issue from the press, all which the people generally are reading; all, indeed, which are asked for by our citizens, which may yield profit and innocent entertainment. And what a privilege is here, that books which very few persons are able to buy to any considerable extent, may thus be furnished in all our homes, without money and without price, for the instruction and the gratification alike of the young and the old. Indeed, next to the institutions of religion and education, our churches and our public schools, no other institution among us can claim preëminence in the people's regard over the public library. The public library is most emphatically what it was first so well called by Edward Everett, the completion of our system of public schools. Why educate your children into the knowledge and the need of books, unless you supply them with books, as they lay aside the text-books of learning and leave the schools?

With these views of the value and importance of a public library, which your committee are happy to find are very generally shared by our citizens, they cannot hesitate to recommend that the town provide, as soon as may be, a suitable building for the safe-keeping and for the well-ordering of their own Library. Such an edifice will be an ornament and an honor to the town. Nine thousand dollars,* it is estimated, would not more than replace the books which are already collected, many of which have been the liberal donation of our own citizens, and of generous persons in other places. A special, commodious, and, as far as may be, fire-proof edifice, will attract, it is believed, more and more the donations of benevolent individuals. It is well known, perhaps, to the citizens, that Mrs. William F. Matchett, of this town, has recently given three hundred dollars for the purchase of a clock for the Library. This large and elegant clock, somewhat unsuited, perhaps, to the present limited apartments, the Trustees are led, for the present, to place there, trusting that an ampler building will before long be ready to receive it.

Few towns, if any, in the Commonwealth surpass our own in the entire collection of commodious, well-ordered, and well-furnished school-houses. And while the neighboring towns are providing, or have already provided, convenient and handsome edifices for their public Libraries, our own town, we are confident, will not consent to be left behind. Your committee are not prepared to-day to present any definite estimates of the expense of a building, nor can they yet recommend a site as, above all others, especially fitted for the erection of the same. In the days allotted them for

---

* Estimate made, it will be observed, in April, 1870.

this report, most of which have been stormy, they have not found it convenient to visit library edifices in other towns, as they would wish to do, or sufficiently to examine building sites on our own streets here. It must be obvious to all that the more free from dust and noise the location for such a building could be, the better. It must be equally obvious that a handsome edifice as contemplated, and for the quiet and elevating purpose for which it is erected, must add very much to the value of real estate in its vicinity. Under this consideration, some have even dared to express the thought that among our citizen land-holders might be found several willing to enroll their names as benefactors to the town by donating a lot for the Library. The valuation of the town is estimated as between five and six millions.* The Boston & Albany Railroad corporation, in the buildings erected and improvements made and now in process, will add about a million to the town valuation. There will be then, by the beginning of the next year, a total valuation of between six and seven millions. The expense of a Library edifice on this entire valuation can add but little, pro rata, to each taxpayer. With these views and suggestions, the committee ask that the subject with which they are charged be recommitted, that at a subsequent town meeting they may present for consideration some particular lot of land which can be had, and the estimated cost of a Library edifice to be erected thereon, should the town see fit so to vote. All which is respectfully submitted in behalf of the committee.

FREDERIC A. WHITNEY.

FREDERIC A. WHITNEY,
LIFE BALDWIN,
WILLIAM WIRT WARREN,
Committee.

Brighton, April 25, 1870.

---

* Valuation now, 1872, between nine and ten millions.

The report was unanimously accepted. Agreeably to the request made therein, it was voted that the subject be recommitted to the same gentlemen, who, taking more time for examination and deliberation, should at a subsequent meeting report again to the town some particular lot, or lots, to be procured, and such specifications as they should be able to present in regard to an edifice.

The committee subsequently met for deliberation on the subject, but do not appear to have been ready to report again, when the warrant for the annual town meeting, March 13, 1871, called their attention in its 12th article in these words: " To see what action the town will take in relation to the purchase of a lot of land, and the erection of a suitable building thereon for the Public Library, and make the necessary appropriation therefor."

And on this the citizens, not at all displeased, it would seem, with their tardy servants, voted unanimously, "That the article be referred to the committee now having the subject in charge, with the request that they report at the next town meeting."

At a town meeting, June 1, 1871, Mr. Life Baldwin, of the committee, submitted and read in the hall the following

REPORT.

The committee appointed by the town to examine and report on the subject of obtaining a suitable lot of land, and erecting thereon a building for the Library, have attended to their duty, and respectfully report: —

That in the annual reports of the Trustees of the Holton Library for the past few years, may be found detailed statements of the cost of the various public library edifices which have been erected in neighboring towns. These reports have been printed and placed in the hands of our citizens, and the committee deem it unnecessary to present the same information therein contained. After examining the facts therein stated, comparing them with other facts procured from citizens of other towns interested in the subject, and comparing, also, the needs of our town with the more or less extensive plans of these other towns, we have come to the conclusion that twenty thousand dollars would be as low a sum as it would be safe to fix upon as the cost of a fire-proof building of the size and completeness necessary to meet the requirements of our town.

The committee have obtained an offer from Mr. Edward C. Sparhawk, to sell a piece of land, being a part of his currant-garden, opposite his dwelling-house, about one hundred and fifty feet wide, and running to Cambridge Street, for a fair price. He declined, however, to name any price for it to the committee.*

The committee have, also, an offer from Messrs. Nathaniel and Samuel Jackson, to sell a piece of land on the east side of Rockland Street, a part of the lot recently purchased by them of L. Baldwin, being one hundred and two feet on Rockland Street, and running back about one hundred and fifty feet, at twelve and a half cents per foot. The committee believe that one half, at least, of the cost of said land can be raised by voluntary contribution.

Mr. Benjamin F. Ricker informed the committee that he would on his part offer a lot of land on Rockland Street, opposite L. Baldwin's estate, on very liberal terms, but could not state the precise terms without consulting Mr. George Wilson, who is part owner of said lot. It may be stated that in case their lot should be selected by the town, Mr. Nathaniel Jackson has offered to pay one thousand dollars

---

* The price was subsequently named by Mr. Sparhawk at twelve and a half cents a foot.

towards its cost, and other parties will also contribute for the same object.

The committee take the liberty of suggesting that in their opinion it would be well for the town to secure a lot of land suitable for a Library edifice as soon as convenient, whatever course may be pursued in regard to building at present.

Respectfully submitted, in behalf of the committee,

LIFE BALDWIN.

FREDERIC A. WHITNEY,
LIFE BALDWIN,
WILLIAM WIRT WARREN,
Committee.

BRIGHTON, May 11, 1871.

The report was unanimously accepted. A motion was then made, "That the town purchase of Messrs. Nathaniel and Samuel Jackson, a piece of land on Rockland Street (east side), one hundred and two feet in front, and running back one hundred and fifty feet, for twelve and a half cents a foot, offered at this low price partly as a donation; that the treasurer be authorized to receive subscriptions towards paying for the same, and to borrow on the credit of the town, and to pay from the town treasury such sums of money as, added to such subscriptions, may be necessary to pay for the same."

An amendment appointing the committee formerly having the matter in relation to the Library edifice in charge, a committee to carry out the provisions of the foregoing motion, was made.

A further amendment was also made, authorizing said committee either to purchase the lot on Rockland Street, of Messrs. Jackson Brothers, or a lot of Messrs. Ricker and Wilson, also on Rockland Street, or *any other piece of land that they might deem suitable for the purpose.* And the motion so amended was unanimously adopted by the town.

The citizens are thus informed of the steps which have been taken towards procuring a lot for a new Library edifice. To the committee having the subject in charge, the town, by its last vote above recorded, has given quite unrestricted power of selection. We trust they will soon be able to mature a plan whereby the building now so imperatively demanded shall be furnished, — a building, let us hope it may be, that, secure from the dust and annoyances of the most frequented streets, combining utility with architectural beauty, shall carry forward the good institution so auspiciously begun; and safely transmit the treasures of knowledge and learning, already accumulated and still increasing, to the generations to come.

Respectfully submitted, in behalf of the Trustees,

FREDERIC A. WHITNEY,
President.

FREDERIC AUGUSTUS WHITNEY,
BELA STODDARD FISKE,
WEBSTER FRANKLIN WARREN, *Librarian and Secretary*,
DAVID TEMPLE PACKARD.

WILLIAM WIRT WARREN,
CHARLES HENRY BASS BRECK,
GRANVILLE FULLER,
JOHN PERKINS CUSHING WINSHIP.

EDMUND RICE,
LIFE BALDWIN, *Treasurer*,
HENRY BALDWIN,
JOSEPH BENNETT,
    Trustees by triennial, biennial, and annual election.

HOLTON LIBRARY, April 1, 1872.

REPORT

OF THE

LIBRARIAN OF THE HOLTON LIBRARY.

To the Trustees:

The Librarian herewith submits the Report for the years ending January 31, 1871, and January 31, 1872.

The number of volumes belonging to the Library, February 1, 1870, the date of the last Report, was	5,838
Number added from February 1, 1870, to February 1, 1872, by purchase, presentation, and binding magazines and pamphlets	2,859
*Total number of volumes to February 1, 1872	8,697
Number of volumes presented between February 1, 1870, and February 1, 1872	397
Total number of volumes presented to February 1, 1872	913
Total number of pamphlets presented to February 1, 1872	1,327
Number of books delivered from February 1, 1870, to February 1, 1872	14,356
Number of days (including evenings) on which the Library has been open during that time (closed for revision most of the time)	79
Average number of books delivered each day	182

* Now something over nine thousand.

Number of books delivered from the opening of the Library in June, 1864, to February 1, 1872,   97,039
Number of days on which the Library has been opened during that time   561
Average number of books delivered each day .   173
Total number of card-holders to August 1, 1870 .   1,853
Number of card-holders from the reopening of the Library, November 1, 1871, to February 1, 1872, three months   592

PERIODICALS.

The following periodicals are received at the Reading-room of the Library. The letters affixed to the titles signify, respectively, w., weekly; m., monthly; 2 m., once in two months; q., quarterly: —

Advocate of Peace. Boston		4to.	m.
Atlantic Monthly. Boston		8vo.	m.
Cornhill Magazine. London		8vo.	m.
Eclectic Magazine. New York		8vo.	m.
Every Saturday. Boston		8vo.	w.
Galaxy. New York		8vo.	m.
Godey's Magazine. Philadelphia		8vo.	m.
Harper's Monthly Magazine. New York		8vo.	m.
Harper's Weekly. New York		fol.	w.
Horticulturist. New York		8vo.	m.
Leslie's Magazine. New York		8vo.	m.
Literary World. New York		4to.	m.
Littell's Living Age. Boston		8vo.	m.
London Punch. London		fol.	w.
New England Historical and Genealogical Register.	Boston	8vo.	q.
North American Review. Boston		8vo.	q.
Old and New. Boston		8vo.	m.
Our Dumb Animals. Boston		4to.	m.
Our Young Folks' Magazine. Boston		8vo.	m.
Religious Magazine and Monthly Review. Boston		8vo.	m.
Scientific American. New York		fol.	w.
The Teacher. Boston		8vo.	m.

The statistics here given apply to the time during which the Library has been open for the delivery of books, from the date of the last report to February 1, 1872, about nine months. The delivery of books was discontinued for the remainder of that time, on account of the preparation of the catalogue recently issued.

The Library was reopened on the first day of November last, partial copies of the catalogue having been obtained from the printers. An entire change has been made, both in placing and numbering the volumes, and in the method of delivery. The plan of numbering by alcove and shelf has been selected as the more advantageous; and the system of placing together works relating to the same general subject, has been adopted.

Each person desiring the use of the Library, signs an application substantially similar to that used by several libraries in our neighborhood, in which application the subscriber gives his residence, and agrees to obey all rules of the Library, and to give immediate notice of any change of residence. All applications are numbered (the numbers corresponding to the cards issued), and are placed on file for reference. A change has also been made in the system of keeping a record of books delivered. By this change we are enabled to tell at a glance the number of times any volume has been taken from the Library, and when and by whom it was taken. These facts will perhaps assist in deciding the troublesome question of duplicates; and will also enable us to furnish many other data in regard to the use of the Library.

The attention of the trustees is respectfully called to the necessity for more ample and suitable accommodations for the Library. Our reading-room has been reduced in size, the space taken from it having been converted into alcoves. This has afforded only temporary relief, as the shelf-room thus obtained is now nearly all occupied; and during the ensuing year the question where to put the volumes that are constantly coming, will again force itself upon us.

The situation of the rooms, the reading-room, particularly, as the trustees' reports have before described, seems hardly appropriate for the purposes for which they are designed. There are disturbances from the basement story, the headquarters of the police, and from the large Town Hall in the story above the Library. The building itself, being of wood, is insecure for the safe keeping of the volumes, many of which are of great value, and, if destroyed, could probably never be replaced. It is undoubtedly impossible to secure suitable conveniences in our present quarters, either for the reading-room, or for the transaction of the ordinary work of the Library, in preparing books for the shelves, and in delivering and receiving the volumes from card-holders. The only remedy for present embarrassment lies in the erection of a new library edifice, as soon as it can conveniently be built.

With the aid of the catalogue just issued, and the bulletin to be kept at the Library, on which are to be entered all new books added, as soon as possible after their reception, every facility seems to be afforded our citizens to become acquainted with the resources of the Library, and to avail themselves of its advantages.

All of which is respectfully submitted,

W. F. WARREN, *Librarian*.

HOLTON LIBRARY, April 1, 1872.

BENEFACTORS[*]

TO THE

HOLTON LIBRARY

BESIDES volumes and pamphlets as below enumerated, other donations have from time to time been made. It has not been found convenient in all cases to record the value of each donation, as suggested in the Rules and Regulations. Gifts from a few of our citizens may be named. At the opening of the Library, Mr. Theodore Matchett caused a life-sized portrait of Mr. James Holton, the founder, to be executed in the highest style of the art, by a German artist of Boston, Mr. F. L. Lay, at a cost of one hundred and twenty-five dollars. The elegant clock, which was duly noticed in the Sixth Annual Report of the Trustees, was presented, at a cost of three hundred dollars, by Mrs. William Frederic Matchett. Mr. John Ruggles presented Bachelder's large and celebrated Isometrical engraving, in colors, in size nearly four feet by three, of the Battle of Gettysburg. The well-executed portrait of President Zachary Taylor was received from Mr. J. P. Cushing Winship. More recently, Mr. George E. Howe has given a very admirable portrait of

---

[*] The Annual Report of the Trustees has always published the donations of the previous year. A complete list of all donations since the opening of the Library having been just prepared for the new Catalogue, it is here inserted, instead of what would naturally be expected, the record, only, of the past two years. All donations made since March last will appear in the Annual List of the Report of February, 1873.

President Grant. A large and handsome photographic picture of the Peace Celebration in this town, in 1865, was likewise presented by Mr. J. P. Cushing Winship. All these are hung in the inner hall. Various Maps and Charts, as enumerated in the catalogue, have likewise been contributed. Mr. Winship, a generous donor from the beginning, has also presented several curiosities and specimens in Natural History as the nucleus for a Museum, for which, it is expected, a suitable room will be prepared in the contemplated new edifice.

JAMES HOLTON'S ORIGINAL BEQUEST, $6,000.

Names and Residence.	Pamphlets.	Vols.
Adams, Blackmer & Lyons, Boston	3	–
Adams, Charles Francis, Quincy	2	1
Alger, Horatio, Rev., South Natick	1	–
Allen, Joseph (D. D.), Northboro'	6	–
Allen, William, East Bridgewater	8	3
American Tract Association, Boston	1	3
American Unitarian Association, Boston	29	51
Anonymous	48	–
Baldwin, Henry, Brighton	7	–
Baldwin, Life, Brighton	22	1
Baldwin, William Henry, Boston	2	–
Bates, Joseph L., Boston	4	3
Baxter, Daniel, Brighton	–	1
Baxter, William, Charlestown	1	–
Bellows, Henry Whitney (D. D.), N. Y.	2	–
Bennett, Joseph, Brighton	5	–
Bigelow, Austin, Brighton	–	2
Blagden, George W. (D. D.), Boston	10	–
Boston Public Library, Trustees of	56	5
Boston School Committee	1	1
Boston School for the Ministry	1	–
Boutwell, George S., Washington, D. C.	78	125
Bowles, Ralph H., Rev., Brighton	4	–
Bradlee, Caleb Davis, Rev., Boston	9	48

Braman, Chandler B., Brighton	–	5
Braman, James C., Boston	3	23
Breck, Charles H. B., Brighton	2	–
Breck, Joseph, Brighton	1	12
Brighton, Town of	–	5
Brookline Library, Trustees of	–	1
Brooks, Charles, Rev., Medford	1	–
Brooks, George M., Washington, D. C.	5	41
Brooks, James, New York	1	–
Buckminster, Lydia, N. H., Framingham	–	3
Capen, Barnard, Boston	–	12
Carter, Artemas, Chicago	–	2
Carter, Artemas, Mrs., Chicago	2	–
Champney, Wm. R., Brighton	2	–
Charlestown Public Library, Trustees of	4	–
Cogswell, James Abbot, Brighton	–	1
Cushman, John P., Rev., Brighton	5	1
Dale, Samuel Holton, Bangor, Me.	–	1
Dana, Esther, Mrs., Brighton	–	2
Dana Library, Cambridge, Trustees of	–	1
Drake, Samuel G., Boston	8	1
Eliot, President, Cambridge	3	1
Everett, Oliver C., Rev., Cambridge	18	–
Faunce, Walter H., Kingston	1	–
Fay, Frank B., Boston	27	–
Fearing, Albert, Boston	35	1
Finotti, J. M., Rev., Brookline, 65 Newspapers	25	7
Fletcher, William I., Waterbury, Conn.	–	1
Fox, George W., Boston	3	–
Fox, Thomas B., Rev., Boston	2	1
Gannett, Ezra S. (D. D.), Boston	18	–
Gill, George L., Quincy	2	1
Greene, Richard G., Rev., Brighton	1	–
Greenleaf, Richard C., Boston	65	22
Hagar, Margaret A., Mrs., Brighton	–	5
Hall, Nathaniel, Rev., Dorchester	20	–
Hammond, Edward H., Brighton	26	–
Harvard University, Cambridge	3	–
Hedge, Frederic H., Rev., Brookline	1	–
Hingham School Committee	1	–
Holbrook, Delia G., Mrs., Brookline	3	1
Holmes, John H., Charlestown	–	1
Hooper, Dwight B., Mrs., Brighton	–	7

Horr, John E., Brookline	1	-
Hosmer, Alfred, M. D., Watertown	5	2
Howe, George Henry, Brighton	-	3
Humphreys, Richard C., Dorchester	1	-
Ilsley, Hosea, Chelsea	3	-
Johonnot, W. H., Boston	5	-
Kidder, Frederic, Boston	-	1
Kirke, George W., Brighton	-	2
Leland, Ira, Rev., Lexington	1	-
Livermore, Isaac, Cambridge	3	1
Lothrop, Samuel K. (D. D.), Boston	9	2
Lowe, Charles, Rev., Somerville	-	2
Manchester Public Library, Trustees of	9	-
Manning, J. M. (D. D.), Boston	1	-
Marshall, C. H., Manchester, N. H.	11	-
Mason, Augustus (M. D.), Brighton	49	-
Massachusetts Bible Society	-	5
Massachusetts, Commonwealth of	-	25
Massachusetts Homœopathic Hospital	1	-
Matchett, Theodore, Brighton	11	23
Matchett, Wm. F., Brighton	18	10
Matchett, Wm. F., Mrs., Brighton	-	4
McKenzie, Alex., Rev., Cambridge	3	1
Mercantile Library Association, Boston	2	-
Mercantile Library Association, N. Y.	2	-
Merchants' Insurance Company, Boston	5	40
Meriam, Emeline, Miss, Brighton	1	-
Minnesota Historical Society	3	-
Mudge, A. & Son, Boston	-	1
Munsel, Joel, Albany, N. Y.	4	2
New Bedford Public Library, Trustees of	-	1
Newcomb, George S., Rev., Quincy	1	-
Newell, Wm., D. D., Cambridge	6	-
Newton, Public Library, Managers of	-	1
Niles, Thomas, Brighton	2	-
Noyes, Chas., Rev., Brighton	1	-
Ordway, J. L., Newton	4	-
Packard, David T., Rev., Brighton	4	-
Palfrey, John G. (D. D.), Cambridge	7	-
Peabody Institute, Danvers, Trustees of	3	-
Peabody Institute, Peabody, Trustees of	5	-
Phillips, Samuel, Brighton	-	1
Pierce, Edward L., Milton	-	1

Pond, Joseph A., Brighton	8	29
Poole, Fitch, South Danvers, now Peabody	1	1
Pratt, Isaac, Brighton	-	1
Putnam, George, D. D., Roxbury	1	-
Quincy, Josiah, Jr., Quincy	2	-
Reading Public Library, Trustees of	2	-
Redwood Library and Athenæum, Trustees of	12	-
Reynolds, Grindall, Rev., Concord, Mass.	1	-
Rice, Abigail, Mrs., Brighton	1	3
Rice, Daniel A., San Francisco, Cal.		1
Rice, Edmund, Brighton	5	8
Rice, Marshall S., Newton	1	-
Robbins, Chandler, D. D., Boston	15	4
Ruggles, John, Brookline	5	63
Sanderson, Eli, Mrs., Brighton	2	1
Sargent, Albert F., Malden	1	-
Sheppard, John H., Boston	2	-
Sibley, John L., Cambridge	3	
Silas Bronson Library, Waterbury, Conn., Managers of	1	-
Silloway, Thos. W., Rev., Brighton	1	18
Smalley, Dan S., Jamaica Plain	1	-
Sparhawk, Edw. C., Brighton, Deed 1, Newspapers 6	20	-
Sparhawk, Rhoda J., Miss, Brighton	1	-
Springfield School Committee	1	-
Stebbins, Alfred, San Francisco, Cal.	-	1
Stebbins, Rufus P. (D. D.), Woburn	2	-
St. Louis Public School Library, Managers of	1	-
Stratton, Henry B., Boston	3	3
Strong, Wm. C., Brighton	-	1
Sumner, Charles, Washington, D. C.	2	38
Swazey, Arthur, Rev., Brighton	2	-
Taunton Public Library, Trustees of	3	-
Thayer, Christopher, Rev., Boston	1	-
Thompson, Wm. R., Rev., Brighton	1	-
Timmins, Thomas, Rev., Brighton	2	-
Torrey, Henry W., Professor, Cambridge	1	-
Turner, Alfred T., Boston	1	2
Tyler, John S., Mrs., Boston	87	9
Waltham Public Library	4	5
Warren, Webster Franklin, Brighton	1	-
Warren, William, Brighton	-	6
Warren, William Wirt, Brighton	4	5
Waterston, Robert C., Rev., Boston	1	-

Watertown, Public Library, Trustees of	2	2
Weiss, John, Rev., Watertown	1	-
Wheildon, Wm. W., Charlestown	-	1
Whiting, William, Boston	-	4
Whitney, Augustus Anson, Cambridge	-	1
Whitney, Edmund Burke, Boston	8	6
Whitney, Frederic A., Mrs., Brighton	6	7
Whitney, Frederic A., Rev., Brighton	141	75
Whitney, Henry Austin, Boston	4	1
Whitney, Solon F., Watertown	1	-
Wight, John B., Rev., Wayland	2	-
Willard, Wm. A. P., Rev., Sudbury	2	-
Willson, E. B., Rev., Salem	1	-
Wilson, Henry, Washington, D. C.	-	3
Winship, Francis Lyman, Brighton	-	3
Winship, John P. Cushing, Brighton, 13 Maps, etc.	165	79
Winsor, Justin, Boston	1	-
Worcester, Public Library, Directors of	5	-
Worcester, Sally, Miss, Brighton	-	1
Worcester School Committee	1	-
Young, Edward J., Rev., Cambridge.	15	-
	1,327	913

SEVENTH ANNUAL REPORT.

LIFE BALDWIN, *Treasurer, in account with* HOLTON LIBRARY.

DR.

1870.		
Feb. 8.	To balance on hand,	$3,485 19
April 21.	" premium on U. S. bond of $100 sold,	9 50
May 20.	" cash of librarian, fines 3 months, ending May 1, 1870,	19 10
June 30.	" coupons due July I, 1870, $99.00, premiums $11.26,	110 26
Aug. 24.	" cash, etc., of librarian, fines three months, ending August 1, 1870,	21 04
Aug. 24.	" cash of librarian, for books lost,	1 31
Sept. 16.	" premium on U. S. bond of $100,	10 25
Oct. 12.	" " " " "	10 12
Nov. 25.	" " " " $200,	18 50
Dec. 28.	" coupons due Jan. 1, 1871, $87.00, premiums $9.24,	96 24
1871.		
Jan. 27.	" premium on U. S. bonds, $600,	49 50
		$3,831 01

CR.

1870.		
March 17.	By cash paid Nichols & Noyes (for books),	$58 66
	Amount carried forward,	$58 66

	Amount brought forward,	$58 66
March 17.	By cash paid W. F. Warren (B. B. Russell's bill),	3 25
April 25.	" " Nichols & Noyes (books),	72 68
April 26.	" " W. F. Warren (F. A. Whitney's bill),	2 50
"	" " W. F. Warren (for books),	4 50
May 20.	" " W. F. Warren (for sundries),	4 36
May 27.	" " Nichols & Noyes (books),	23 23
"	" " Harris & Eeles (binding books),	14 85
July 18.	" " Noyes, Holmes & Co. (books),	102 52
Aug. 24.	" " W. F. Warren (Anna Glover's bill),	4 00
"	" " W. F. Warren (J. L. B. Pratt, for book),	5 00
"	" " W. F. Warren (bill of sundries),	5 06
Sept. 8.	" " Noyes, Holmes & Co. (books),	27 36
Sept. 16.	" " Suffolk Ins. Co. (renewal of policy),	60 00
Oct. 12.	" " Noyes, Holmes & Co. (books),	124 63
Oct. 26.	" " W. F. Warren (W. B. Towne's bill),	12 00
Nov. 26.	" " Noyes & Holmes (books),	171 91
	Amount carried forward,	$696 51

		Amount brought forward,		$696	51
Dec.	15.	By cash paid W. F. Warren (Mrs. Brabiner's bill),		8	50
"	"	" W. F. Warren (F. A. Whitney's bill, books),		7	19
1871.					
Jan.	24.	" " W. F. Warren (F. H. Tubbs' bill),		1	50
Jan.	27.	" " Crosby & Damrell (books),		68	00
"	"	" Noyes, Holmes & Co. (books),		648	17
Jan.	31.	By balance of account. U. S. bonds $2,300, cash, $101.14,		2,401	14
				$3,831	01

To the trustees of Holton Library :

  Respectfully submitted by

        L. BALDWIN, *Treasurer.*

JANUARY 31, 1871.

EIGHTH ANNUAL REPORT.

Life Baldwin, *Treasurer, in account with* Holton Library.

Dr.

1871.
Feb. 2.	For balance on hand, as by last report,	$2,401 14
	For cash of town treasurer for unexpended balance of town appropriation for 1870,	360 89
May 23.	For premium on U. S. bond of $100,	13 75
June 19.	" " " "	14 37
26.	For coupons due July 1, 1871, $63, prem. $7.87,	70 87
Aug. 23.	For premium on U. S. bond of $100,	13 12
Nov. 21.	" " " $200,	30 00
1872.		
Jan. 1.	For coupons $54, prem. $4.86,	58 86
		$2,963 00

Cr.

1871.
Feb. 2.	By cash paid librarian (W. H. Piper & Co.'s bill),	$34 24
14.	Paid Noyes, Holmes & Co. (books),	155 07
Mar. 24.	" " " "	89 38
April 17.	" " "	109 41
May 16.	" " " "	82 41
16.	By cash paid stamps for checks,	50
	Amount carried forward,	$471 01

	Amount brought forward,	$471	01
May 16.	By cash paid librarian (selectmen, Brown & Co.'s bill),	12	00
June 15.	By cash paid librarian (D. C. Colesworthy's bill),	2	00
15.	By cash paid librarian (E. H. Hammond's bill),	3	90
15.	By cash paid librarian (Massachusetts Teachers' Association),	8	25
15.	By cash paid Noyes, Holmes & Co. (books),	151	21
Aug. 23.	By cash paid Noyes, Holmes & Co. (books),	142	40
23.	By cash paid librarian (F. H. Tubbs' bill),	2	62
23.	By cash paid A. Williams & Co. (books),	1	05
Sept. 23.	By cash paid Noyes, Holmes & Co. (books),	38	43
Nov. 21.	By cash paid Noyes, Holmes & Co. (books),	160	18
Dec. 12.	By cash paid Noyes, Holmes & Co. (books),	61	35
1872.			
Jan. 15.	By cash paid Noyes, Holmes & Co. (books),	102	17
	Balance,	1,806	43
		$2,963	00

Respectfully submitted.

L. BALDWIN, *Treasurer.*

BRIGHTON, Feb. 1, 1872.

NINTH ANNUAL REPORT

OF THE

TRUSTEES

OF THE

HOLTON LIBRARY,

BRIGHTON.

FEBRUARY 1, 1873.

BOSTON:
ALFRED MUDGE & SON, PRINTERS, 34 SCHOOL STREET.
1873.

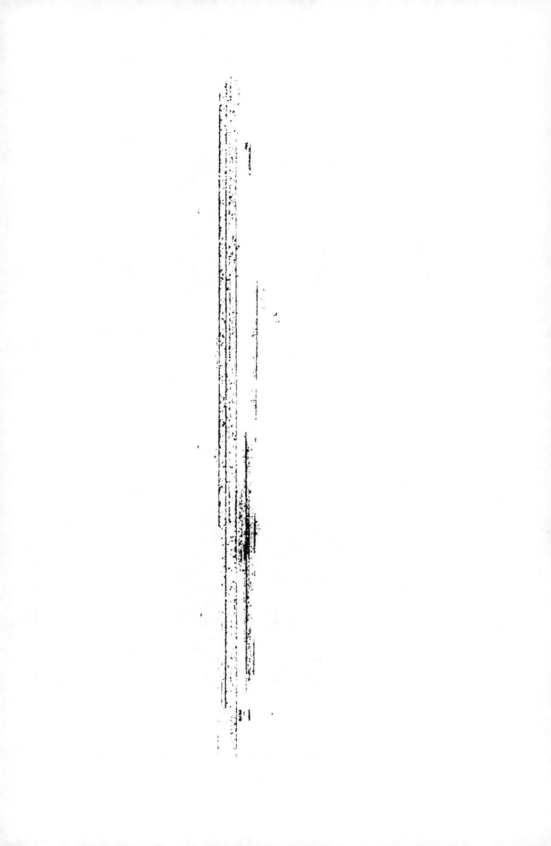

NINTH ANNUAL REPORT

OF THE

TRUSTEES

OF THE

HOLTON LIBRARY,

BRIGHTON.

FEBRUARY 1, 1873.

BOSTON:
ALFRED MUDGE & SON, PRINTERS, 34 SCHOOL STREET.
1873

TOWN OF BRIGHTON.

HOLTON LIBRARY, February 1, 1873.

TO THE AUDITORS:

Gentlemen, — I have the honor to transmit to you, herewith, the ninth Annual Report of the Trustees of the Holton Library, prepared in obedience to the ordinance adopted by the town, April 8, 1864.

Yours respectfully,

W. F. WARREN,
Secretary of the Board of Trustees.

TRUSTEES

Of the Library from its Commencement.

	Elected.	Ret'd.
BALDWIN, HENRY	1872	
BALDWIN, LIFE	1864	
BENNETT, JOSEPH	1870	
BENTON, ABNER INGALLS	1866	1868
BICKFORD, WEARE DOW	1864	1872
BRECK, CHARLES HENRY BASS	1867—	
CUSHMAN, JOHN PAINE	1864	1866
FISKE, BELA STODDARD	1865	1870
" " "	1872	
FULLER, GRANVILLE	1864	
HUTCHINSON, CHARLES CARROLL	1864	1865
JACKSON, NATHANIEL	1864	1869
MATCHETT, THEODORE	1864	1867
MATCHETT, WILLIAM FREDERIC	1867	1872
PACKARD, DAVID TEMPLE	1869	
* POND, JOSEPH ADAMS	1864	1867
RICE, EDMUND	1865	
RUGGLES, JOHN	1864	1865
WARREN, WEBSTER FRANKLIN	1869	
WARREN, WILLIAM WIRT	1864	
WHITNEY, FREDERIC AUGUSTUS	1864	
WINSHIP, JOHN PERKINS CUSHING	1864	

* Deceased, October 28, 1867.

OFFICERS

Of the Library from its commencement.

PRESIDENTS.

	Elected.	Retired.
JOHN RUGGLES,	April 18, 1864 — October 9, 1865.	
FREDERIC AUGUSTUS WHITNEY,	November 13, 1865 —	

SECRETARIES.

JOHN PERKINS CUSHING WINSHIP,	April 18, 1864 — March 13, 1865.
BELA STODDARD FISKE,	March 13, 1865 — March 14, 1870.
WEBSTER FRANKLIN WARREN,	March 14, 1870 —

TREASURER.

LIFE BALDWIN,	May 23, 1864 —

LIBRARIANS.

JOHN PERKINS CUSHING WINSHIP,	June 13, 1864 — July 9, 1866.
WEBSTER FRANKLIN WARREN,	July 9, 1866 —

PRESENT LIBRARY SERVICE.

WEBSTER FRANKLIN WARREN, *Librarian.*
MISS MARY JANE BOWKER, *First Assistant.*
MISS CLARA ADELIA WENTWORTH, *Second Assistant.*

THE special attention of parents and guardians of the young is called to the following law of the Commonwealth : —

" Whoever wilfully and wantonly writes upon, injures, defaces, tears, or destroys any book, plate, picture, engraving, or statue belonging to any law, town, city, or other public library, shall be punished by a fine of not less than five dollars, nor more than one thousand dollars, for every such offence."

NINTH ANNUAL REPORT

OF THE

TRUSTEES OF THE HOLTON LIBRARY.

In obedience to the ordinance respecting the Holton Library, adopted by the town of Brighton, April 8, 1864, the Trustees have the honor to submit their ninth annual

REPORT.

They have watched the institution entrusted to their charge, with unabated interest and satisfaction, through another year. Entering upon the tenth year of its organization, it has well realized the expectations of its friends; largely outgrown, in the number of its books, many similar establishments throughout the country of prior date, and is felt more and more in our community as a vital force.

PAST REPORTS.

In the series of reports thus far issued, the trustees have presented quite fully such suggestions for the well-ordering of the library, and adopted such measures as our own circumstances seemed to require, and the wise counsels and experience of similar libraries to commend. Accordingly, the present report needs but briefly to allude to the condition, prospects, and wants of the institution. They cannot, however, refrain, in this connection, from expressing their gratitude to their fellow-citizens for a very willing co-operation; for a ready acquiescence with recommendations made through the annual reports; for generous appropriations and for general patronage and support.

REPORTS OF THE TREASURER AND LIBRARIAN.

Mr. Life Baldwin and Mr. Webster F. Warren, who have served faithfully in these important departments, through another year, will furnish the usual statistics. According to the terms of bequest, a portion of the fund originally donated by the founder, Mr. James Holton, is annually expended for books, in addition to appropriations made by the town. The number of volumes has steadily increased during the year, by purchase and by donation. It is certainly highly creditable to the librarian and his assistants that so small a percentage of loss in books has been incurred in so large a library and with so general a circulation. In the annual examination, two volumes, only, have as yet failed to appear. Including the pamphlets arranged in cases, partially bound, catalogued as volumes, and ready for use in the reading-room, the number exceeds, a little, ten thousand.

RULES AND REGULATIONS AMENDED.

Some important changes have been made, the past year, in the rules and regulations. A large and expensive catalogue of the books having been furnished (1872), including the rules and regulations, names of officers, — Dictionary of Pseudonyms, donations with names of donors, from the establishment of the library, together with Bulletin No. I, it was deemed best that a nominal charge should be made for copies of the same. Copies of the first catalogue of the Holton Library (1866) had hitherto been furnished gratuitously. Accordingly, at a regular meeting of the trustees, held April 8, 1872, due notice of the proposed amendment having been previously given, Article 13, Chapter H. of the Rules and Regulations, which read thus: "Catalogues of books belonging to the Holton Library, with the established Rules and Regulations annexed, shall be provided by the trustees, and on application, a copy shall be given to the head of each family," was altered by striking out all after the word, "trustees," and inserting the words "to be furnished, gratuitously, or otherwise, at their discretion, to the head of each family."

A small charge is now made for each copy of the catalogue delivered from the Librarian's desk.

The desire having been generally expressed, that the library should be opened on each secular day of the week, a second amendment was adopted at a special meeting of the trustees held, pursuant to notice, December 17, 1872.

It was voted, "That Article 1, Chapter II, of the Rules and Regulations be struck out, and the following adopted in place thereof."

"The library shall be opened every day, from three to six o'clock, and from seven to nine o'clock, P. M., except Sundays, and on such evenings as the trustees meet, when only the outer hall shall be opened to the public for the delivery of books. No books, however, shall be delivered for two weeks immediately preceding the fifteenth day of August."

And a third amendment relating to the subject of fines for the retention of books, was made necessary by the daily opening of the library.

At the regular meeting of the trustees, January 13, 1873, it was voted, "That the last clause of Article 5, Chapter II, of the Rules and Regulations, which reads as follows: 'The fine for retaining any volume beyond the time above specified (fourteen days) shall be five cents for every half week of such retention,' should be amended by striking out the words 'five cents for every half week of such retention,' and inserting in place thereof 'two cents for every additional day of such retention, Sunday excepted.'"

THE DAILY OPENING OF THE LIBRARY

Has given much satisfaction. Indeed it has been contemplated to open daily as soon as the new edifice was prepared. More room for general purposes, and special accommodation for newspaper stands in the reading-room, will there be furnished, and so, necessarily, the place must be more frequented. Still it has been wise thus to anticipate the new building. The card-holders have appreciated the privilege of wider choice in days and more frequent resort to the halls. Such as peruse the various magazines and periodicals and books of reference at the tables, can now read more continuously. And though the wear and tear of books must be somewhat increased by more frequent loaning, still, we are satisfied greater advantages on the whole are secured.

ERASE FROM CARDS NUMBERS NOT WANTED.

Some card-holders neglect to do this. See what trouble comes from the omission. A card is presented at the desk bearing several numbers. Suppose one of these is of a book which the bearer has just read, but which has not been erased. The assistant must bring from the alcoves the first book *in* which is marked on the card. It may chance to be the very book which the bearer read last week, and has not erased its number. The assistant does not know this. The assistant, before handing the book to the applicant, must stamp the slip corresponding to the book with the day of the month which has been already set in the little machine for that day. The applicant then receives the book, but to find that it is not wanted. What next? Probably the request, "Can't you change this book?" Shall the assistant, whose duty, let it be observed, has been correctly discharged, take back the book, undo the work of the machine (which is really entering a book as returned, which has not been out, that day), and proceed to the alcoves for the next book *in*, which stands on the card? The slip of this book must then be stamped for the day before the book is handed to the applicant. It might appear that this second book, likewise, was one recently read, and not erased. Meanwhile other applicants are waiting in order for their books. Hence, in libraries generally, has come the rule, —

BOOKS NOT CHANGED ON THE DAY OF DELIVERY.

This is not a capricious rule, but most important. Of course, if the assistant has made an error, the book must be changed. But if the card-holder has presented numbers of books not wanted, which numbers should have been erased, it is inevitable that such applicant must bear for a day the inconvenience, if the work of the library is to be conducted on system, and the right of other applicants waiting their turns is to be regarded. Indeed, card-holders will observe printed on one side of their card, "Erase all numbers of books not wanted."

LABOR AND SERVICE IN THE LIBRARY.

We cannot be insensible to the fact, that with the growth and more frequent opening of the library, the labor in its care and management is more than proportionally increased. Desirable books from among the many that daily issue from the press, must be watched for and selected. Not a few, but many different departments of literature must be kept supplied. Classifying and cataloguing the books has, especially with the few past years, become, as it were, a science. The covering, labelling, repairing, and binding is constant work. The delivery and the return-checking of books, though well systematized here, demands diligent care to prevent errors. The preparation of bulletins to supplement the large catalogue, must now be a continuous task, since card-holders are impatient to learn of the latest arrivals of books. The different languages, the various idioms in which titles of books are now expressed, the frequent use of pseudonyms often so ludicrously confounded in catalogues with the real names of authors, all these considerations are continually rendering less competent for the essential part of the library service those persons who are masters only of the English tongue. Indeed, the best public libraries of to-day have been as far elevated above the ordinary circulating libraries of New England, thirty and forty years ago, as have our present public schools since Horace Mann, about as many years since, inaugurated those wonderful reforms in popular education, which, not without some storms of obloquy and reproach on his devoted head, have ripened into the glorious harvest of to-day. Would we maintain the rank which our library has gained among kindred institutions of the Commonwealth, it can only be done by the same ready appropriations which have thus far been given, by the strict observance of every wise regulation for the well-ordering of the same, by the faithful and devoted labors of each person engaged in the library service.

The trustees would remark, in this connection, that although no formal rules have been thus far enacted regulating the intercourse between the card-holders and the assistants employed in the library, still it is to be understood that conversation on matters irrelevant to the delivery and return of books is out of place here. No intelligent card-holder can fail to see that occupying the minds of the assistants while on duty, with various topics of friendly conversation, is so far unfitting them for the best performance of their duties. We think the directors of our banks and insurance offices would regard much visiting by friends in banking hours, much conversation with the employees on matters not concerning the institution, as very objectionable. Let the same be so regarded here.

While the assistants are liable at any moment to be called on by some new-comer for the delivery or return of volumes, it is hardly their province to select books for card-holders who have failed to make any selection for themselves, by numbers entered on their cards. Let it be remembered that the assistants in the library, with the work of repairing and covering books, which is never a finished work, and with all their other duties, have enough to occupy all their time. At the meeting of the trustees, last month, it was enacted, in view of the additional work to be imposed by the daily opening of the library, "that the librarian be authorized to employ such assistance as he may deem necessary in order to carry out the purposes of the vote, subject to the approval of the library committee." We are sure that the faithful librarian, already so fully occupied with various public offices and cares, will personally agree with us, in desiring here, in these halls, no unnecessary interruption in the time and work of those whom he employs. It will be well if, without formal enactments, all visiting the library in the established hours, will regard that the services to be rendered by all the assistants is service paid for from the town treasury. Let it be considered that each five or ten minutes taken in the outer hall, by one or another visitor, though in most kindly chitchat respecting the last sleigh-ride, or the last or the coming ball, may not only cause mischief in library entries, figures, accounts, through the delicate brain-work of agreeable assistants, but is actually defrauding the town of time and devoted service, for which it must pay; a transaction, after all, not much more honorable than other frauds.

We have recently lost the services of one of our best assistants, Herbert Langdon Waterman, of this town, who has been long employed here, and who, in addition to good scholarship, was giving us the fruits of well-improved experience. Edwin Osgood Kimball, also of this town, second assistant, has likewise left, the past year, to engage in commercial pursuits. Miss Sarah Jane Bowker, third assistant, who has been steadily employed here since 1870, is promoted to the place of first assistant to the librarian, and is acquiring considerable facility in the work of cataloguing. Miss Clara A. Wentworth, of this town, who was subsequently in the library service while the large catalogue was in preparation, has just resumed work here, attending chiefly to the delivery and return of books. The president of the trustees gives such portion of his time as he can devote to the work of selecting, classifying, and cataloguing the books.

DONATIONS.

In the report of the trustees, last issued, was given a complete summary of all donations of books, pamphlets, newspapers, maps, and charts, with all other bequests and gifts, made to the library since its establishment, with all names of donors. The number of the volumes thus bestowed was nine hundred and thirteen, and of pamphlets, one thousand three hundred and twenty-seven. The librarian, in his present report, resumes the publication of the annual donations. The list will be found to embrace esteemed and honored names, from abroad as well as at home. Our senators and representatives in Congress, Hon. Charles Sumner, Hon. Henry Wilson, Hon. George M. Brooks, Hon. Constantine C. Esty, Hon. William Whiting, have made numerous and valuable presentations. From the latter gentleman, a resident of Boston Highlands, has come one of the most elegantly executed volumes of the American Press, printed but not published, the work, *con amore*, of the honored donor, entitled, "Memoir of Samuel Whiting, D. D., and of his wife, Elizabeth St. John; being genealogy of both families with reference to their English ancestors, and American descendants. Fifty copies printed, not published."

Books and pamphlets have been given by several ladies, as by Miss Sally Worcester, of Boston, Mrs. Ellen P. Minot and Mrs. Delia Ann Holbrook, of Brookline, Mrs. William F. Matchett, of Boston, Miss Maria L. Huntley, of Lancaster, Miss Maria C. Perkins and Mrs. F. A. Whitney, of this town. President Charles Wm. Eliot, of Harvard University, Rev. Dr. Peabody, likewise of the University, in a large and rich collection of his own works; and Mr. John L. Sibley, Librarian at the University; Rev. Dr. Stearns, President of Amherst College; Rev. Abiel Abbot Livermore, President of the Meadville Theological School; Rev. Alexander McKenzie, of Cambridge, and Rev. Edward J. Young, Professor in the University there; Rev. Dr. Allen, of Northboro; Rev. Augustus Woodbury, of Providence, R. I.; Rev. Charles T. Brooks, of Newport, R. I.; Rev. Linus Parker, of New Orleans, La., and Rev. Charles H. Brigham, of Ann Arbor, Mich., have made donations.

Rev. Caleb Davis Bradlee, of Boston, whose gifts to our library have been so valuable and frequent, stands credited on the list of last year with twenty-one volumes, twenty-five pamphlets, and one hundred and one newspapers, donated. Rev. Edward I. Galvin, Pastor of the First Church here, Unitarian Congregational, though a citizen of the town but a few months, has manifested, certainly, one sure trait of the good citizen, — a lively interest in the Public Library of his adopted town, — and sent to its alcoves forty-eight volumes and fifty-two pamphlets. Among them are the works of Archbishop Tillotson, a London edition of 1728, in three volumes, folio, with portrait; the New Testament in Greek, two volumes, octavo (Griesbach's edition), thus enabling us to count in the library admirable copies of the New Testament in the English, French, German, and Greek tongues, and of the Bible, in all those languages but the last. Donnegan's large and valuable Greek and English Lexicon, and Boyer's French Dictionary; Sermons, with Memoir and Portrait of the sainted Buckminster, of Boston, are likewise comprised in Mr. Galvin's collection; also, Hutchinson's Xenophon, the Cyropædia, or Institution of Cyrus, in handsome Greek type; Upham's Intellectual Philosophy; Paley's Moral and Political Philosophy, a London edition, in two volumes; several works published in London and in Holland, in Latin and in English, literary curiosities, from the respective dates of their publication, in 1604, 1649, 1694, and 1695. A good number of modern works, likewise, accompany the ancient in this donation; and among the half hundred pamphlets (many of rare value and interest) are comprised a considerable number of the works of one of America's ripest and most charming scholars, William Henry Furness, D. D., of Philadelphia.

Former ministers of the First Church, here, have sent contributions to the library, the past year, as Mr. McDaniel, the monthly paper which he edits so well, at Cambridge, entitled, "The Light of Home," Mr. Timmins, and Mr. Whitney. It has been pleasant to record tokens of remembrance from some who long lived here, known and esteemed, now removed, — as from the daughter of the distinguished Noah Worcester, D. D., who died here, Miss Sally Worcester, now of Boston, who, at the advanced age of eighty-two years, sits with sightless eyes, but with a soul all light with patience and submission, with divinest faith and peace; from Mr. John Ruggles and Mrs. Holbrook, of Brookline; Mr. Francis A. Hall and Mr. Wm. H. Baldwin, both of Boston.

The names of our citizens will be noticed, as of Joseph Breck & Son, Wm. C. Strong & Co., Francis L. & J. P. C. Winship, Samuel Phillips, J. M. Hawks, M. D., Frank W.

Standish. Names before on our list of donors, as also names of first contributors, we observe, as of Hon. Albert Fearing, Mr. and Mrs. Wm. F. Matchett, Richard C. Greenleaf, Hon. Nathaniel B. Shurtleff, Edmund B. Whitney, Wm. W. Greenough, Justin Winsor, John F. Elliot, Henry B. Stratton, George W. Fox, Charles Reiche & Brother, all of Boston. Hon. Stephen Salisbury, of Worcester, and Samuel S. Green, of Worcester, George H. Whitman, of Billerica, Charles Francis Adams, Jr., and Geo. L. Gill, of Quincy, Alfred Hosmer, M. D., of Watertown, Hon. Mathew Carpenter, of U. S. House of Representatives, Benjamin H. Rhoades, of Newport, R. I., Noah L. Wyeth, M. D., of Cambridge, E. K. Johnson, of Nahant, Edward Appleton, of Reading, John N. Genin, of New York, and various publishing houses of Boston, New York, and Philadelphia, have contributed.

Contributions have come from the public libraries of Boston, Brookline, Charlestown, Chelsea, Gloucester, Lowell, Manchester, N. H., Melrose, Milton, Nahant, Newton, Quincy, Reading, Taunton, Waltham, Watertown, Worcester; from the Redwood Library and Athenæum, at Newport, R. I.; from Harvard University, Amherst College, and the Meadville Theological School, and from the Mass. Bible Society. Donations are regularly received from the various U. S. departments at Washington, from the Massachusetts State departments, from the Boston School Committee, Auditor, etc.; from the American Peace Society, from the Society for the Prevention of Cruelty to Animals, from the American Unitarian Association, from the Hingham Agricultural and Horticultural Society, from the Mercantile Library Associations of New York and of Philadelphia, from the Library Company of Philadelphia, from the Mechanics Association of Gardiner, Me., from the Royal Nursery of Ghent, Belgium, from the Cobden Club, and other associations of London. Other donations not here named may be seen in the Librarian's report. The total number for the year is two hundred and five books, five hundred and forty-one pamphlets, and one hundred and seventy-four newspapers.

A SPECIAL DONATION FROM THE TRUSTEES.

The trustees have directed the insertion in this report of the following correspondence which stands on their records, and which will be found to explain itself: —

BRIGHTON, December 12, 1872.

TO THE REV. FREDERIC A. WHITNEY,
President of the Holton Library.

DEAR SIR: Understanding last summer that you designed altering your house, in order to increase the size of your study, the trustees of the Holton Library considered it a suitable occasion to acknowledge in a slight degree their appreciation of your services as president of the board, in rearranging the books, and preparing a catalogue which has elicited much praise in the care and ability displayed. They desire further, that this may be a record of the esteem they entertain for one who, during a long series of years, has merited and received the regards of his fellow-citizens.

In accordance with the foregoing sentiments, at a meeting of the trustees, the undersigned were appointed a committee to obtain and present to you the accompanying book-cases, table-desk, and chair.

They have appreciated your devotion to the work entrusted to your care, which, having been gratuitously rendered, has caused a large pecuniary saving to the town. They trust that the gift now presented may prove as pleasing to you as the opportunity of presenting it is agreeable to the trustees.

Hoping that we may have for many years, the benefit of your co-operation and assistance in matters promoting the prosperity of the library, and wishing you heaven's choicest blessings, we remain, with sentiments of high esteem, very truly and sincerely yours,

J. P. C. WINSHIP,
WM. W. WARREN,
EDMUND RICE,
Committee.

GARDNER STREET, BRIGHTON, Dec. 17, 1872.

To MESSRS. J. P. C. WINSHIP, WILLIAM W. WARREN, EDMUND RICE, *Committee of the Trustees of the Holton Library.*

GENTLEMEN: For the rich and valuable gift which, in behalf of the trustees, you have presented to me, I desire to return my warmest thanks. The pair of massive and elegant book-cases, the table-desk, and the chair, which you have so thoughtfully and generously furnished, seem to me among the finest specimens of the art. You are pleased to associate the donation with such services as I have been able to render in behalf of the Holton Public Library, and particularly in the late preparation of the catalogue. I am most happy that my humble efforts may be thus connected with an institution which has been so auspiciously inaugurated, and which promises so well for the growing intelligence and enjoyment of our community.

Your munificent present will continually remind me of the pleasant intercourse shared both with the present and the past members of the board of trustees; and I fondly hope that our united endeavors may be still further blessed in the growing prosperity of our library, and in the consequent diffusion of knowledge and virtue among our people.

With warmest regards to yourselves, gentlemen, and to my other esteemed associates on the board, I remain,

Your obliged servant,

FREDERIC A. WHITNEY.

LIBRARY ENDOWMENTS.

We have presented, in former reports, numerous endowments, gifts, and legacies for public libraries, in various towns and cities. Two or three may be added here, which have come to our notice among the many, doubtless, of the past year, of which we have not learned.

Col. Elijah Hale, of Stow, who died last fall, among other bequests, has endowed a public library there. Brevet Brigadier-General Sylvanus Thayer, of the United States Engineer Corps, died at his home and birthplace, in Braintree, Mass., in September last. Giving to Dartmouth College, of which he was an alumnus, sixty thousand dollars, to the Boston Public Library, two hundred valuable volumes, besides rare European scientific manuscripts, he bequeathed thirty thousand dollars to found a public library in his native town. Miss Arabella Rice, who died in Portsmouth, N. H., last fall, giving out of an estate of six hundred thousand dollars more separate legacies to relatives, and to charitable and benevolent associations, than has often been done, bestowed thirty thousand dollars for a public library in Kittery, Me., the birthplace of her father, adjoining Portsmouth. Far better, we deem it, to spread before the public, through suitable channels, intelligence like this, than the revolting records of crime in which our daily prints abound.

BULLETIN NO. TWO OF THE CATALOGUE

Has been prepared, and will be ready directly for the citizens. It will be found to embrace a good proportion of the desirable books which have been published since the issue of Bulletin No. 1. In all the departments of the library, valuable accessions have been made. The alcoves are overcrowded. There being no further convenient shelf-room against the walls, or space for the erection of more fixed alcoves, some large movable book-cases, no longer in use at the president's study, have been temporarily located in the inner hall. By congressional enactment, a public library, having ten thousand volumes, is entitled to receive, freely, all the publications of the Smithsonian Institution at Washington. These valuable acquisitions it will now be the fortune of this library to possess. By reason of the increase, an additional policy of insurance has just been negotiated on the books and on the costly clock.

CONCLUSION.

Finally, in confident assurance of the great advantages accruing to our community from this institution, the trustees commend it to the fostering care and the widest improvement of the citizens. They trust that the next report of the board will detail its establishment in the new edifice with all needed facilities for its most successful management and continued increase. In the good prospect of the approaching annexation of our town with Boston, they see grounds to expect its yet wider usefulness as a branch of the City Public Library. That noble institution, the pioneer of most of the public libraries in our land is, each year, prospering more and more, under the judicious watch of its president, Mr. Greenough, and trustees, its incomparable superintendent, Mr. Winsor, with his successful co-workers, Messrs. Wheeler, Whitney, Capen, and others. The *Alma Mater*, as it were, of these many smaller libraries, she has already stretched out her motherly arms and embraced as branches of her sturdy stock, those at East Boston, at South Boston, and at Roxbury. These libraries all, these good books reaching all classes, are the divinely-appointed means of the nation's redemption and life. The handmaids of intelligence, virtue, religion, they silently upheave the mighty masses of error, superstition, sin. In the old burial-ground at Cambridge, in front of the University grounds, was long shown a tree, that first shooting out as a simple twig from a cleft in a rock, had at length through growing mass and strength lifted a tombstone from its bed. So from the gentle diffusion of knowledge and good learning, from the favoring influence of books, is thought awakened, — are nobler impulses stirred and higher aims reached; and the mightiest masses, behind which sin and death were entrenched, are overthrown. Gather in your public libraries, good books! Give them freely, as water to the thirsty, as bread to the hungry. The grand old prophet Isaiah still speaks to us as to the chosen people; and in no tame prose, but in his own matchless Hebrew verse, as he stamped it on the roll which became a Bible's sacred page: —

"Ho, every one that thirsteth, come ye to the waters!

"Even ye that have no money, come ye, buy and eat.

"Yea, come buy wine and milk,

"Without money and without price.

"Wherefore do ye spend your money for that which is no bread,

"And your substance for that which doth not satisfy?"

Respectfully submitted, in behalf of the Trustees,

FREDERIC A. WHITNEY,
President.

FREDERIC AUGUSTUS WHITNEY,
BELA STODDARD FISKE,
WEBSTER FRANKLIN WARREN, *Librarian and Secretary,*
DAVID TEMPLE PACKARD.

WILLIAM WIRT WARREN,
CHARLES HENRY BASS BRECK,
GRANVILLE FULLER,
JOHN PERKINS CUSHING WINSHIP.

EDMUND RICE,
LIFE BALDWIN, *Treasurer,*
HENRY BALDWIN,
JOSEPH BENNETT,

Trustees by triennial, biennial, and annual election.

HOLTON LIBRARY, February 1, 1873.

REPORT

OF THE

LIBRARIAN OF THE HOLTON LIBRARY.

To the Trustees:

The Librarian herewith submits the ninth Annual Report for the year ending January 31, 1873.

The number of volumes belonging to the Library, February 1, 1872, was	8,697
Number of volumes added from February 1, 1872, to February 1, 1873, by purchase and by binding magazines and pamphlets	701
Number of volumes presented to the Library	205
* Total number of volumes, February 1, 1873	9,603
Increase of volumes during the year	906
Number of pamphlets presented, February 1, 1872	1,327
Number of pamphlets presented, from February 1, 1872, to February 1, 1873	541
Total number of pamphlets added to, February 1, 1873	1,868
Number of newspapers presented, from February 1, 1872, to February 1, 1873	174
Number of card-holders, February 1, 1872 (that number having signed from November 1, 1871, to February 1, 1872, on the reopening of the Library, three months)	592

---

* The Library now comprises, with pamphlets arranged in cases, partially bound, catalogued, and ready for use at the Reading-Room as books, something over ten thousand volumes.

Number of card-holders, from February 1, 1872,
to February 1, 1873 373

Number of card-holders, February 1, 1873 . . 965
Number of books delivered, from February 1, 1872,
to December 19, 1872 15,709
Number of days, including evenings, on which the
Library has been open during the above-named
time 92
Average number delivered each day of that period, 171
Number of books delivered from December 19,
1872, to February 1, 1873, forty-three days . 3,011
Number of days, including evenings, on which the
Library has been open, from December 19, 1872,
to February 1, 1873 37
Average number delivered each day of that period 81

PERIODICALS.

The following periodicals are received at the Reading-Room of the Library. The letters affixed to the titles signify, respectively, w., weekly; m., monthly; 2 m., once in two months; q., quarterly: —

Advocate of Peace. Boston	4to.	m.
Atlantic Monthly. Boston	8vo.	m.
Cornhill Magazine. London	8vo.	m.
Eclectic Magazine. New York	8vo.	m.
Every Saturday. Boston	8vo.	w.
Galaxy. New York	8vo.	m.
Godey's Magazine. Philadelphia	8vo.	m.
Harper's Monthly Magazine. New York	8vo.	m.
Harper's Weekly. New York	fol	w.
Horticulturist. New York	8vo.	m.
Leslie's Magazine. New York	8vo.	m.
Literary World. New York	4to.	m.
Littell's Living Age. Boston	8vo.	w.
London Punch. London.	fol.	w.
New England Historical and Genealogical Register. Boston	8vo.	q.
North American Review. Boston	8vo.	q.
Old and New. Boston.	8vo.	m.
Our Dumb Animals. Boston	4to.	m.
Our Young Folks' Magazine. Boston	8vo.	m.
Religious Magazine and Monthly Review. Boston	8vo.	m.
Scientific American. New York	fol.	w.
The Light of Home. Cambridge	4to.	m.
The Massachusetts Teacher. Boston	8vo.	m.

BENEFACTORS

TO THE

HOLTON LIBRARY.

For a complete list of all donations of every description made to the Library since its establishment in 1864, with the names and residences of all donors, see the Catalogue, pp. 309–14; also the same copied into the Trustees' Report of last year, 1871–72.

FOR THE YEAR 1872–73,

And the number of volumes, pamphlets, newspapers, etc., received from each.

JAMES HOLTON'S ORIGINAL BEQUEST $6,000.

Names and Residence.	Pamphlets.	Vols.
Adams, Charles F., Jr., Quincy	1	–
Allen, Joseph, D. D., Northboro	1	–
American Peace Society, Boston, 12 Newspapers.		
American Unitarian Association, Boston	28	2
Anonymous, 7 Newspapers	4	–
Appleton, D. & Co., New York	1	–
Appleton, Edward, Reading	1	1
Bennett, Joseph, Brighton	2	–
Bicknell, A. J. & Co., New York	1	
Boston Public Library, Trustees of	5	2
Boston School Committee		1
Bradlee, Caleb Davis, Rev., Boston, 101 Newspapers	26	22
Breck, Joseph, Brighton		1
Breck, Joseph & Son, Brighton	6	1
Briggs & Brother, Rochester, N. Y.	1	–

Names and Residence.	Pamphlets.	Vols.
Brigham, Charles H., Rev., Ann Arbor, Mich.	1	-
Brighton, Town of	-	3
Brookline, Public Library, Trustees of	1	-
Brooks, Charles T., Rev., Newport, R. I.	-	1
Brooks, George M , Hon , Washington, D. C.	1	18
Campbell, James, Boston	2	-
Carpenter, Matthew, Hon., Washington, D. C.	3	-
Carter (James), Dunnett & Beale	1	-
Chandler, Charles F. & Wm. H., New York	1	-
Charlestown Public Library, Trustees of	1	1
Chelsea Public Library, Trustees of	-	1
Cobden Club, London, Eng.	8	2
Denham, A. & Co., New York	1	-
Drake, Samuel G., Boston	1	..
Eaton, John, Jr., Washington, D. C.	-	1
Eliot, Charles Wm., President Harvard University	-	1
Eliot, John Fleet, Boston	-	8
Esty, Constantine C., Hon., Washington, D. C.	-	1
Everett, Oliver, Rev., Cambridge	4	-
Fearing, Albert, Hon , Boston	7	2
Fox, George W., Boston	4	-
Fox, Thomas B., Rev., Boston	2	1
Galvin, Edward Illsley, Rev., Brighton	52	48
Gardiner Mechanics Association, Me.	1	-
Genin, John N., New York	-	1
Gill, George L., Quincy		
Green, Samuel, Worcester	1	
Greenleaf, Richard C , Boston	13	5
Hall, Francis A., Boston	23	-
Hawks, J. M. (M. D.), Brighton	-	1
Hingham Agricult. & Horticult. Soc.	1	
Holbrook, Delia A., Mrs., Brookline	10	1
Hosmer, Alfred, M. D., Watertown	8	2
Houtte, Louis Van, Ghent (Belgium)	1	-
Huntley, Maria L. Miss, Lancaster	-	1
Hurd & Houghton, Cambridge	1	-
Johnson, E. K. Mr., Nahant	-	1
Kidder, Frederic, Boston	-	1
Library Company of Philadelphia (The)	-	1
Lippincott, J. B. & Co., Philadelphia	6	-
Little, Brown & Co. Messrs., Boston	-	1
Livermore Abiel A., Rev., Pres. Meadville Theo. School, Pa.	1	-

Names and Residence.	Pamphlets.	Vols.
Lowell City Library, Trustees of	13	–
Maclean, Stoddart & Co., Philadelphia	–	1
Macmillan & Co., Oxford, Eng.	1	–
Manchester Public Library, N. H., Trustees of	1	–
Mass. Bible Society, Boston	–	5
Mass Peace Society, Boston, 12 Newspapers.		
Matchett, Wm. F. Mr., Boston	21	3
Matchett, Wm. F. Mrs., Boston	–	1
McDaniel, Samuel W., Rev., Cambridge, 12 Newspapers.		
McKenzie, Alexander, Rev., Cambridge	2	–
Melrose Public Library, Trustees of	1	–
Mercantile Library Association, New York	–	2
Mercantile Library of Philadelphia	6	1
Minot, Ellen P., Mrs., Brookline	34	
Newton Free Library, Managers of	3	
Noyes, Holmes & Co., Boston	–	1
Parker, Linus, D. D , New Orleans, La., 1 Newspaper.		
Peabody, Andrew P. (D. D.) (Harvard University)	35	2
Perkins, Maria C., Miss, Brighton	68	
Phillips, Samuel, Brighton	4	
Potter, Thomas B., London, Eng.	8	1
Quincy Public Library, Trustees of	1	–
Reading Public Library, Trustees of	1	
Redwood Library Athenæum, Newport, R. I.	1	–
Reiche, Charles & Brother, Boston	–	1
Rhoades Benjamin H., Newport, R. I.	–	1
Ruggles, John, Brookline	–	1
Salisbury, Stephen, Hon., Worcester	1	–
Scribner & Co., New York, 8 Newspapers.	1	–
Sheppard, John H., Boston	2	–
Shurtleff, Nathaniel B. (M. D.), Boston	1	–
Sibley, John L., Librarian, Harvard University	1	1
Smith, Alfred R., London, Eng.	7	
Society for Preventing Cruelty to Animals, 12 Newspapers.		
Standish, Frank W., Brighton	–	1
State Board of Health of Mass.		1
Stearns, William A. (D. D.), President, Amherst College	1	4
Stevens, Joseph L., Jr., Gloucester		1
Stout, George H., New York, 1 Newspaper.		
Stratton, Henry B., Boston	3	3
Strong, Wm. C. & Co., Brighton		1
Sumner, Charles, Hon., Washington, D. C.	5	16

Names and Residence.	Pamphlets.	Vols.
Sweet, George H. & Co., New York, 8 Newspapers.		
Taunton Public Library, Trustees of	3	–
Teele, A. K., Rev., Milton	1	–
Timmins, Thomas, Rev., Brighton	1	–
Tourjée, Eben, Boston	1	–
Turner, Alfred T., Boston	–	1
U. S. Patent Office, Washington, D. C.	31	–
Van Sicler, Henry K., New York	2	–
Walsh, Ann, Brighton	–	1
Warren, James L. L. F., San Francisco, Cal.	2	–
Whiting, Wm., Hon., Boston Highlands	–	1
Whitman, George H, Billerica	1	–
Whitney, Edmund B., Boston	2	4
Whitney, Frederic A., Mrs., Brighton	1	1
Whitney, Frederic A., Rev., Brighton	11	14
Whitney, Solon F., Watertown	1	–
Winship, F. Lyman, Brighton	1	–
Winship, J. P. Cushing, Brighton	12	4
Winsor, Justin, Boston	1	–
Woodbury, Augustus, Rev., Providence, R. I.	1	1
Worcester Free Public Library, Trustees of	2	–
Worcester, Sally, Miss, Boston	–	1
Wyeth, Noah L. (M D.), Cambridge	12	1
	541	205

All of which is respectfully submitted.

W. F. WARREN,
Librarian.

HOLTON LIBRARY, February 1, 1873.

NINTH ANNUAL REPORT.*

L. BALDWIN, *Treasurer, in account with* HOLTON LIBRARY.

DR.

1872.
Jan. 16.	For balance on hand,	$1,806 43
Mar. 13.	" premium on $200, U. S. bonds sold,	23 50
April 13.	" premium on $100, U. S. bonds sold,	12 62
May 18.	" fines from librarian, to May 1, 1872, as per statement,	29 21
July 1.	" coupons due July 1, 1872, $45 00, premium $6.14,	51 14
Aug. 21.	" premium on $100, U. S. bonds sold,	15 00
Sept. 30.	" fines from librarian, to Aug. 1, 1872,	23 87
Nov. 29.	" premium on $200, U. S. bonds sold,	30 50
Dec. 27.	" coupons due January 1, 1873, $36.00, premium $4.37,	40 37
1873.		
Feb. 13.	" premium on $100 bond sold,	15 50
		$2,048 14

1872. CR.
Mar. 13.	By cash paid Noyes & Holmes, books,	$49 04
	" cash paid A. Williams & Co., books,	68 48

* For sums of money appropriated by the Town for support of the Library, apart from the Holton Fund, see report of the Town Treasurer.

April	9.	By cash paid Noyes, Holmes & Co., books,	$60 68
"	13.	" cash paid Noyes, Holmes & Co., books,	82 29
May	16.	" cash paid W. F. Warren, bill of sundry articles,	12 38
"	17.	" cash paid Noyes, Holmes & Co., books,	52 11
Aug.	9.	" cash paid Sampson, Davenport & Co., books,	4 00
"	"	" cash paid W. F. Warren, books,	3 00
"	21.	" " " Noyes, Holmes & Co , books,	130 83
Sep.	30.	" cash paid W. F. Warren, stationery,	7 12
Oct.	2.	" cash paid Noyes, Holmes & Co., books,	44 23
Nov.	29.	" cash paid Noyes, Holmes & Co., books,	183 71
1873.			
Feb.	13.	" cash paid Noyes, Holmes & Co., books,	164 87
"		" Balance on hand, U.S. bond, 1,100 00 cash in bank, 85 40	1,185 40
			$2,048 14

Respectfully submitted to the Trustees of Holton Library by

L. BALDWIN, *Treas.*

BRIGHTON, Feb. 13, 1873.

CPSIA information can be obtained
at www.ICGtesting.com
Printed in the USA
BVHW041200110219
539965BV00013B/59/P